The Ministry of Reconciliation

The Ministry
of
Reconciliation

A commentary on the order of penance 1974

J.D. Crichton

Ordo paenitentiae translated by Geoffrey Webb

This translation is for study purposes only

Distributed in the United States by

CHRISTIAN CLASSICS

205 Willis Street, Westminster, Md. 21157

SILVER LAKE COLLEGE LIBRARY
2406 SOUTH ALVERNO ROAD
MANITOWOC, WI. 54220

A Geoffrey Chapman book published by
Cassell & Collier Macmillan Publishers Ltd.
35 Red Lion Square, London, WC1R 4SG
and at Sydney, Auckland, Toronto,
Johannesburg,
an affiliate of Macmillan Inc. New York.

ISBN 0 225 66075 X

Nihil obstat: R. J. Cuming DD, Censor
Imprimatur: David Norris *v.g.*,
Westminster, 10 September 1975

Printed in Great Britain by
The Camelot Press Ltd, Southampton

Contents

Preface

For many centuries the sacrament of penance has played a very important part in the lives of Catholics. All have used it, the high and the low, the poor and the rich, the intelligent and the not so intelligent and, if asked, most of them would say that they could not have led any sort of Christian life without it. It is significant, however, that one unconsciously uses the past tense. Is this still happening? The answer is, to a great extent, yes. But many observers have noted a falling off in its use in recent years though it is not always easy to say why. We may hazard the guess that in the recent past people went to confession too frequently and this was no doubt a hangover from the days when they (mistakenly) thought they *always* had to go to confession before communion. In that case, and given the steadily increasing number of communicants, the decline is not significant. But there seems also to be a certain disaffection from the use of penance and there is enough evidence to show that here there is reason for concern. Whether the new Order of Penance will do anything to ameliorate that situation, time alone will tell, but, though it has been long delayed, it may well have come just at the right moment. It will force us to think about the sacrament of penance and since it is (still) a prominent part of pastoral practice, it may lead us to re-think our pastoral methods. If so, it will be doing what the other revised rites are slowly forcing us to do. Liturgy and life cannot be separated.

I find I have written twice before on penance and in this book I have been concerned not to repeat myself, though inevitably I have done so. I find too that in the course of the commentary I have raised certain theological questions, for instance about the nature of sin and of the obligation to confess mortal sins auricularly, especially before receiving holy communion. It may be thought that I was going beyond my brief. But consideration of these and one or two other related matters is necessary even in a liturgical commentary, for the decisions eventually reached on them will inevitably affect the liturgy and practice of penance. We are, it would seem, in an interim stage and if the other rites which have been revised and promulgated by the church authorities in recent years cannot be said to be definitive for all time, *a fortiori* this is true of the Order of Penance. Meanwhile, let us be grateful for what we have been offered. It is much to be hoped that we shall be allowed a period of true, controlled and informed experiment, for in the process I believe we shall learn a great deal about the needs of the people and of the exigencies of the sacrament of penance.

I am grateful to Father Geoffrey Webb for his translation of the Order, which will be found in the second part of the book.

J. D. C.

Feast of St Augustine of Canterbury, 1974

It should be noted that the translation of the Ordo Paenitentiae *provided in this book is unofficial and is intended for the purposes of study only. The competent authority will, in due course, issue a translation for use in public worship.*

NOTE

The Question of the Translation of 'ad valorem sacramenti', OP 33.
It has been pointed out (E. Matthews, *Clergy Review*, May, 1975, p. 334; K. Donovan, *The Month*, July, 1975) that '*ad valorem*' does not necessarily mean 'for validity'. On the other hand, the 'White Book' of the ICEL translation has 'validity'.

At first sight, the critics seemed to be right but on re-reading the text I am not so sure. It is necessary to take into account the *whole* paragraph which states the 'dispositions and conditions' required of the penitent if his use of Public Reconciliation is to be 'profitable'. These include true sorrow, reparation of any scandal or harm he has caused and the resolve to confess his sins individually 'in due time'. It is common teaching that these 'dispositions' are required for the validity of the sacrament: e.g. no repentance, no forgiveness. In other words, the phrase '*ad valorem*' does not refer simply to subsequent confession but to the whole complexus of dispositions and conditions.

As to the question of subsequent confession, Father Matthews usefully points out that what is required is that the penitent shall *intend* to confess 'in due time' and here he is close to the Order: '(he must) *resolve* to confess in due time'. As Father Matthews rightly observes, if this is made clear, we shall avoid false crises of conscience.

In the light of all this, the remarks on p. 91 are too absolute and should be corrected. The matter is correctly stated on p. 58.

As to the reason why '*ad valorem*' instead of '*ad validitatem*' was used, this must remain a matter of speculation until there is some official clarification. The Editor of the *Clergy Review* (August, 1975) suggests that '*ad valorem*' means something like 'fruitfulness'. But particularly in the sacrament of Penance it is difficult to distinguish 'validity' from 'fruitfulness'. It may well be that the revisers wished to avoid the more legalistic term.

CHAPTER ONE

Penance and Life

If baptism, marriage and the eucharist can be seen as related to human living, it is less easy to relate penance, with its complexus of notions, sin, repentance and expiation, to the events of ordinary life. It is true that people do have a sense of wrong-doing, though this may be no more than emotional, and they seek forgiveness. After a marital row husband and wife seek forgiveness and reconciliation but this is a purely inter-personal event and, unless they are Christians, has (usually) no reference to God. Expiation, on the other hand, seems to have been a constant feature of non-Christian religions, though it was usually and perhaps always a merely external affair, not involving the conscience. It was the counterpart of sin regarded as the breaking of a ritual law, involving technical uncleanness, and expiation was merely the removal of the uncleanness. The reason for this state of affairs is that sin and repentance are *biblical* concepts. What is too little remembered is that they are part of revelation and we should not know what sin and repentance are but for the teaching of the Bible. The ordinary Greek word for 'sin' (*hamartia*) means 'missing the mark' and Socrates seems to have thought that sin consisted of ignorance. You sinned because 'you did not know'. The Greeks, in fact, were not very sin-conscious, and that no doubt is why the people of the Renaissance found release from the sin-ridden atmosphere of the late Middle Ages in following them.

At a deeper level of human existence, however, people experience suffering, anguish, a sense of failure and a feeling that they have taken a wrong turning. Such experiences may not come close to a sense of sin, but they are symptoms of a rift in the human condition, evidence that right-doing, even with the best will in the world, is countered by the drive of the personality to wrong-doing.[1]

[1] Rom. 7: 14–20.

It may seem exaggerated to say that every human life is a tragedy, for some are remarkably tranquil, but it is not too much to say that on the longer view every human life has tragic elements. There is the constant dying that we may live, the dying to childhood that we may come to maturity, the dying to self that we may truly love, the dying to this life that we may enter into a fuller and unending life. All this involves suffering, confrontation with the forces outside us and with the urges of our nature inside us. As Job said and St Leo liked to repeat, *militia est vita hominis super terram* (human life in this world is a battleground). In conflict, in fact, are the forces of life and death, the one warring against the other, and the issue hangs in doubt until the end.

It is against this background that some[1] see the 'tragedy' of the passion, death and resurrection of Christ. He in his own person was acting out the human tragedy, the conflict between sin and goodness, between life and death, and by his resurrection showed that life has overcome death and that every human life can share in his victory. To the eucharist, Rahner goes on, we bring our experience of the tragedy of life and through it are able to enter on another stage where the battle continues to be fought out. The same must be true of the sacrament of penance which is to be seen as an act of the tragedy where reconciliation is achieved. Just as people bring to the eucharist their experience of conflict and suffering, so in penance they bring precisely their 'broken-ness' (contrition), which for the moment has flawed or seemed to ruin their lives, so that through repentance, the turning of themselves back to the Good, they may, by the power of Christ, be healed, set on the right way once again and reconciled.

This, it is true, is to raise the whole matter to the Christian order of things and that alone is an indication of how difficult it is to speak of repentance without reference to Christ. But it is sufficient to show that there is a meeting point between life and penance.

Confirmation that penance is relevant to life comes from what might be thought to be an unexpected quarter. It has been pointed out[2] that there is an interesting and intended parallel between the *Constitution on the Church in the Modern World* and

[1] See K. Rahner in J. D. Crichton, *Christian Celebration: the Mass* (Geoffrey Chapman, 1972), p. 162.

[2] LMD (1967, 90): J. Badini, 'La Constitution "Paenitemini" dans la ligne du Concile'.

2

certain passages in the papal constitution *Paenitemini*. The first speaks of the desire of the church, after scrutinising its own nature, to address itself not only to its own children but to all who call upon the name of Christ and indeed to the whole of mankind. The Council turns its attention to human society and to the world 'which is the theatre of man's history and carries the marks of his energies, *his tragedies*, and his triumphs; the world which the Christian sees as created and sustained by its Maker's love, fallen indeed into the bondage of sin, yet emancipated now by Christ. *He was crucified and rose again to break the stranglehold of personified Evil* so that the world might be fashioned anew according to God's design and reach its fulfilment.'[1]

The document *Paenitemini* repeats many of these phrases, addresses 'all men of our times' and links the matter of penance to the progress of the world: 'The Church has considered more attentively its role in the earthly city, that is to say, its mission of showing man the right way to use earthly goods and to collaborate in the "consecration of the world".' Within this context it reminds Christians of the need for restraint in the use of material goods lest they 'be delayed by the things of this world in their pilgrimage towards their home in heaven'.[2] This might seem to be a surprising conclusion. The modern world is organised for consumption and even waste, and the doctrine of *Paenitemini* needs completing by the teaching of the *Constitution on the Church in the Modern World* on the dignity of man, who is the end-purpose of any social order, and on the right use of created goods. What is certain is that in a world that is apparently committed to the production of ever more consumer goods, the Christian has the obligation to assess the value of life and to struggle to preserve its quality. This may very well demand restraint, what *Paenitemini* calls 'abstinence', and this will be the modern way of 'mortification' or self-denial. This too is a theme that is to be found both in the *Constitution on the Church in the Modern World* and in *Paenitemini* itself.

The pope in this latter document appeals with all the more confidence to men of goodwill because he finds that the church has noted that 'almost everywhere and at all times penitence has held a place of great importance in non-Christian religions and is closely linked with the intimate sense of religion which pervades

[1] *Const. Church Mod. World* (2); Abbott & Gallagher (eds), *Documents of Vatican II* (Geoffrey Chapman, 1966), p. 200,
[2] *Penitence* (C.T.S. trans. of *Paenitemini*), p. 4.

the life of most ancient peoples as well as with the more advanced expressions of the great religions connected with the progress of culture'.[1] Judaism and Islam are examples that spring to the mind. It may be that there are radical differences between the Christian and non-Christian views of penitence, but the pope thinks that there is enough in common to make the comparison valid. All penitence, with the fasting and prayer that accompany it, can be seen as medicinal in that it delivers man from slavery to his instincts and as a stage towards a closer union with God.

But the pope has another perspective also. '"Repent and believe in the Gospel" . . . constitute, in a way, a compendium of the whole Christian life.'[2] But further, it is the vocation of the church to hold up the values of the gospel before the world and, the pope is saying, that means that there must be a penitential element in the life of every Christian as well as in the proclamation of the gospel if this is to be achieved.

All this may seem a far cry from the sacrament of penance, at least as it is conceived and practised nowadays. Like many another liturgy, it has been cut off from life, from the continuing life of the individual Christian, from the life of the church and from life *tout court*. One reason for this is that it has become an individual act performed in the darkness of a confessional. Another and more important one, is that sin, largely on account of legalistic notions, has been thought of as an individualistic breaking of the law. Again, and in spite of the constant teaching of the church, the Christian life, seen as a living with Christ in the mystery of his passion, death and resurrection, has been regarded as something existing *alongside* penance rather than as an integral part of it. *Paenitemini* states traditional doctrine when it says that by baptism the Christian is committed to the living out in his own experience of the paschal mystery: 'The sacrament (baptism) configures him to the passion, death and resurrection of the Lord and places the whole future life of the baptised under the seal of the mystery' (p. 7). The Order of Penance takes up this teaching in what is indeed one of its more important statements. Baptism and penance are related: 'The first victory over sin is shown in baptism when we are crucified with Christ that "this sinful body" may be destroyed and we may be delivered from slavery to sin (Rom. 6: 6). Risen, however, with Christ we can

[1] *Op. cit.*, p. 5.   [2] *Op. cit.*, p. 6.

4

henceforth live for God. . . . But further, Christ committed a ministry of penance to his church, so that Christians who have fallen into sin after baptism may be renewed in grace and be reconciled with God.'[1] Thus is returned to currency a notion that was prominent in all early liturgy and the teaching of the Fathers.[2]

Even in its teaching on frequent confession the Order states that it is to be seen as a constant effort to renew the grace of baptism, so that while we bear in our bodies the death (*mortificationem*) of Christ, his life may be more clearly manifested in ours.[3]

As we shall see in greater detail below, the Order also re-establishes the relationship between penance and the church: it is 'reconciliation with God and the church' and 'by penance Christians obtain pardon from the mercy of God and at the same time are reconciled with the church which they have damaged by their sins. The church in turn, by love, example and prayer collaborates in their conversion' (OP 5, 4). It remains to be seen how even the revised rite can help ordinary Christians to relate the sacrament of penance to their lives.

The solution of this problem is largely a matter of teaching. The heavy individualistic attitude towards sin and repentance will have to be corrected and means must be found to bring this sacrament back to the centre of the ordinary Christian's consciousness. It is well known that there has been a widespread disaffection towards the sacrament for long enough, especially among the young who have complained that the sacrament *as practised* has no relevance to *their* life and that the whole procedure seems unrealistic to them.[4] The corrective in outlook will be found partly in the Order—penance is an ecclesial act, i.e. an action of the whole church—but there will have to be a considerable change not only in confessional practice but also

[1] OP2. The passage concludes with a quotation from St Ambrose: 'The church has water and tears, the water of baptism and the tears of repentance.' Eph. 41: 12, PL, 16, 1164.

[2] The prayer adapted by the Order for the Lenten penitential service (App. II: 13) from the Gelasian Sacramentary has this theme, which is to be found in St Ambrose, as the references in the Order itself make plain.

[3] II Cor. 4: 10 and OP 7b.

[4] The evidence is considerable. Two samples may be mentioned: Sister Laurence Murray, *Confession: Outmoded Sacrament?* (Geoffrey Chapman, 1972); Mary Hallaway, 'The Sacrament of Penance: A Lay View' in *Penance: Virtue and Sacrament*, ed. John Fitzsimons (Search Press, 1969), pp. 9–22.

5

in the organisation of ecclesiastical life if the sacrament is to be embedded in ordinary living. As with the eucharist, so with penance there will have to be a discovery of the sense of community, of the solidarity of Christians not only in grace but in sin. Concern for the church-community will be an indispensable element in the restoration of penance to the centre of people's interest. But that is not enough. The Christian community must demonstrate its concern for the wider community in which it lives, seeking especially to bring reconciliation where there is tension and dispute. No more than any other part of the liturgy is penance a merely ritual act. It is related to life and, just as we have learnt that we must bring our daily living to the eucharist, so we shall have to learn that we must bring our faults, both private and public, our daily repentance and our desire to reconcile, to the celebration of the sacrament of penance. We have learnt that the offering of our life in the eucharistic becomes 'valuable' through its union with the self-offering of Christ; we shall have to learn also that all the penitential element of our lives is actualised in the sacrament of penance.[1] Here we meet the forgiving, reconciling Christ who takes the whole of our repentance and penitence to himself, transfuses it with his love and makes it effective of pardon and reconciliation. As the Order puts it, the sinner returns to the Father 'who first loved us' (I John 4: 19), to Christ who gave himself up for us (Eph. 5: 2, 25) and to the Holy Spirit who is generously poured out on us through Jesus Christ our Saviour (Tit. 3: 6) so that we are able to respond with love.

As for community, we shall have to see the relevance of penance to social life, as we have begun to see the relevance of the eucharist to it. You cannot with a good conscience take bread and wine and consecrate them if you are indifferent to a starving world. Likewise, you cannot express your sense of hurting others or of failing others if there are no 'others' to express it to. Only if the church-community is identifiable in the anonymous society of our time as a Christian community of forgiveness and reconciliation will it be able to bear witness to the reconciling mission of the whole church.[2] This last, says the pope, is the very heart

[1] This is relevant to the difficult matter of 'satisfaction'. If there is an element of penitence in the life of the Christian whether *before* or after confession, it becomes operative through the action of Christ in the sacrament.

[2] See M. Winter, *Mission or Maintenance* (Darton, Longman & Todd, 1973), for certain views on the local Christian community.

6

of the gospel message[1] which will be conveyed—or not—by the local community. Here, at this point, the services of penitence envisaged by the Order should be most effective.

Finally, there is the matter of sin and of confessing sins. As the studies of Sister Murray and Mary Hallaway mentioned above, as well as many others, have shown, the 'sin-grid' with its corresponding 'laundry list' has deadened the sense of sin and, on account of extreme categorisation, has unduly limited people's awareness of the range of sin. As well as the uncomprehending and unsympathetic attitude of confessors, this is the main burden of young people's complaints about the practice of the sacrament. They, like all of us, are involved in situations which have plus and minus values and given current practice in the examination of conscience and the confessor's expectations of what people should say (and no more!), they find it difficult to the point of impossibility to expound the state of their consciences.[2] It is true that the Council of Trent said that mortal sins must be confessed in kind, number and circumstances, but the last seems to have to be used only to determine whether a sin was of a particular kind or not. This of course has its importance but if 'circumstances' could be translated 'situation' the penitent or many of them would find 'going to confession' a more profitable exercise than it is at the moment.

For a new and better practice of the sacrament, therefore, it will be necessary to re-examine the nature of sin and to recast the examination of conscience. This will have to be based on a deeper notion of sin, a matter to which we shall have to return. There are of course problems here and I do not wish to give the impression that in my view all in the current practice is wrong. Catholics have had a realistic understanding of what is sinful and what is not and this has saved them from vagueness on the one hand and scrupulosity on the other. But whatever the difficulties about the formation of a new theology of sin and if, given human necessity, we cannot get away from categories and codes, law, in a word, we must at least stop seeing sin as *simply* the breaking of a code. The extraordinary amount of positive law the Catholic had to live under until recently did

[1] *Paenitemini, trans. cit.*, p. 6.
[2] For further observations, with evidence, see Sister Murray's book and the essay of Mary Hallaway, referred to above; and also the present writer's two essays in *Penance: Virtue and Sacrament* and Chapter 11 of *Christian Celebration: the Sacraments* (Geoffrey Chapman, 1973).

ill service to a deeper understanding of sin. The breaking of a church law, e.g. failure to abstain from meat on Fridays, was too easily put on a par with an infringement of the natural and divine law, e.g. adultery. Nominalist notions that things are wrong because they are forbidden and not vice versa was more prevalent than was always realised.

We cannot of course expect that a new Order of Penance, which is basically a liturgical document, will or can put all these things right. But its theology is rich enough to provide a basis for a new catechesis of penance which is urgently needed.

There is a wider question: how can the doctrine of this Order or of *Paenitemini* be conveyed to the modern world? If the church is a penitential church, can we hope to persuade anyone to become involved in it? It is a very large question which needs a great deal of thought. But perhaps that is the wrong way to put the matter. The whole burden of these two documents is that the church is a forgiving, reconciling community and once you say 'forgiveness' or 'reconciliation' you are immediately involved in difficult and painful decisions. Even human forgiveness is not an easy matter and reconciliation at the human level demands a willingness to *give* on both sides. 'Forgiving' as well as 'giving' are painful, penitential; perhaps if the church can be seen as a forgiving and reconciling community, it will be possible to persuade people of the need for penitence.

CHAPTER TWO

The New Order of Penance

The long-awaited *Ordo Paenitentiae* appeared on 2 December 1973 'by special mandate of the supreme pontiff' over the signatures of Cardinal Villot of the Secretariat of State and Archbishop Bugnini, secretary of the Congregation for Worship.[1] Its first words set the keynote of the whole document: '*Reconciliationem inter Deum et homines.* . . . By the mystery of his death and resurrection Jesus Christ effected reconciliation between God and men. . . .'[2]

The sacrament that for too long has been called 'confession' and in which oddly enough the 'absolution' ('getting an absolution') received enormous emphasis is the sacrament of reconciliation, reconciliation of man with God, of the sinner with the church and of man with man. But the sacrament itself is part of a wider ministry of reconciliation which Christ committed to his church (I Cor. 5: 18 ff). This is effected by the preaching of the Good News of salvation and by baptising men and women with water and the Holy Spirit.

Thus, right at the beginning of this Order, the Decree sets forth the truth that the whole church is the place of reconciliation between God and man. If this is true it follows that the

[1]Vatican Press, 1974. The present writers do not know why it was promulgated over the signature of Cardinal Villot. Perhaps it was because there was no president of the Congregation for Worship at the time. But the statement 'by the special mandate of the supreme pontiff' is something new, and no similar statement appears in any of the other new liturgical documents. However, the Secretariat of State did issue a special statement at the time of the promulgation of the *Orde Unctionis Infirmorum* and one can only suppose that the Holy See wishes to indicate that its full authority is engaged in the promulgation of liturgical documents. In view of the opinions expressed in the Catholic press, such statements would seem to be necessary.

[2]The scripture text referred to is in full: 'When we were reconciled to God by the death of his Son, we were still enemies; now that we have been reconciled, surely we may count on being saved by the life of his Son' (Rom. 5: 10).

church is as much a reconciling community as it is a eucharistic community and in fact both functions are combined in the Mass. But there is the fact of human sin. Christians 'abandon their first love' (Ap. 2: 4) and sever their friendship with God. For this reason Christ instituted the special sacrament of penance (John 20: 21–23) which in different ways the church has celebrated ever since. Penance is a *special* ministry of reconciliation and whatever forms it has taken throughout the centuries, this remains true.

What then is the particular significance of this term? First of all, it represents the older way of thinking when the discipline of penance was fully operative. Repentance came at the beginning of the process (though no doubt it was deepened during the time of penance); satisfaction was made over a period of time with a view to reconciliation; and reconciliation with God and the church was the climax of the process and marked the moment when the penitent could once again enter into full and visible unity by celebrating the eucharist. It could be said that reconciliation actualised the sinner's repentance, took up into itself his satisfaction and expressed and effected what was later called absolution.

It can also be said that reconciliation underlines more clearly the action of God in the sacrament. Repentance is the response of *man* to God but, we are told, the Bible frequently uses the term to indicate that God reconciles man with man and this is obviously appropriate to the sacrament that reconciles sinners with the church, the assembly of God's people.

But, as the Order says elsewhere, the notion it wishes to emphasise above all is that penance, like all the sacraments but in a particular way, is an encounter between God and man: 'Reconciliation better expresses the bilateral encounter which is proper to the sacraments; God comes to meet man with his gift of salvation, operative through Christ who is active in the church, and man, likewise in the church, receives into himself by faith the same gift of salvation from God.'[1] This doctrine is worked out and expressed in a variety of ways throughout the Order.

But this notion of reconciliation would seem to have a wider relevance. It can perhaps best be expressed by recalling the three-point programme of the Taizé community in France:

[1] The above three paragraphs owe much to the article of F. Sottocornola in *Notitiae*, Feb. 1974 (90), p. 67.

reconciliation of man with God, reconciliation of the Christian churches and reconciliation of man with man. The first is covered by the ministry of reconciliation within the church, the second by the ecumenical effort and the third? This is the problem. If the church is the place of reconciliation, it is necessary that it should appear to be so and yet it does not. In recent years the church has been a place of contention: the conservatives launch accusations of heresy against the progressives who often go on their way light-heartedly ignoring the feelings of the conservatives. There is too little *intellectual* charity in the church, too little willingness to enter into other people's minds, too great a desire to have everyone *thinking* the same way. What members of the same church share is *faith*, not thought, and faith, as we are beginning to learn, can be expressed in a variety of ways and still remain the same faith. There has been contention with authority and if it is to the credit of authority that on the whole it has been pacifying, it has not yet reached the point of reconciliation which involves a real meeting of minds and hearts, a willingness to understand and a desire to achieve a harmony without sacrifice of principle.

If, then, the ministry of reconciliation is to become a reality in the life of the church, it will, like all liturgy, have to be taken outside the church precincts and become a formative element in the lives of Christians. If it is taken seriously, it may well be more difficult to 'go to confession' than it has been in the past and ordinary Christians who have sometimes refused to receive holy communion after a bad family row have had the roots of the matter in them. The Order contains a deep and far-reaching doctrine and it will be necessary to propagate it by all the means at the church's disposal.

The Reform of the Rite

In a former book the present writer sketched out what he believed to be the principles that any reform or penance would have to be built on if it was to be faithful to the brief statement in the Constitution (72) and to the pattern of reform of all the other sacraments. They can be put under four heads:[1]

a Liturgy is an act of the church, i.e. of the gathered people: 'it is not a private function' (CL 26b).

[1] See *Christian Celebration: the Sacraments*, p. 211.

b There must always be a proclamation of the word of God.
c The rite must be visible for such is the nature of liturgy (CL 7).
d It must be of such sort that the people as a community can participate in it.

If we look over the whole range of rites provided in the Order we can say that in one way or another these principles have been implemented. This can be seen from the contents of the Order. There we find the following:

I The Order for the Reconciliation of Individual Penitents;
II The Order for the Reconciliation of Several Penitents with Individual Confession and Absolution.
III The Order for the Reconciliation of Several Penitents with General Confession and Absolution.
IV Various models of services of penitence for different occasions and categories of people.

The last three items certainly satisfy our second principle, (b). They are simply Bible Services though with different features and they satisfy the first principle, for they are impossible without a community of people. So the needs of (d) are met too. In as far as they are public services they are visible rites (c) though in II the sacramental act is private. Looking over the whole material one can say that III is the model rite for in it *all* the requirements of the Constitution are met. In presenting the sacrament of penance whether in liturgical catechesis or in any other teaching situation there is a great deal to be said for taking this as the model. The fulness of the liturgy of penance will then be made plain. The first rite, which will be the one most familiar to people I, has also incorporated the principles as far as they are compatible with the nature of private confession. There is a proclamation of the word, however brief, and the acts of confession, the declaration of sorrow and the absolution are sacramental signs even if only the penitent and confessor are aware of them. We have to conclude that what could be done has been and this statement is not to be read as a grudging admission of the fact. Private or individual penance has been with us for centuries, it has proved to be fruitful in many ways and no one with any sense would want to abolish it. But one may be allowed the guess that if the other ways of reconciliation are also allowed to exist in the church, the individual practice of penance will be transformed.

CHAPTER THREE

The Ministry of Reconciliation

The life of Christ was massively a ministry of reconciliation. All the rest is a matter of means, of how mankind may enter into that reconciliation. We believe so that we may be saved, that is reconciled; we worship so that through the reconciling Christ we may give praise and thanksgiving to God. The church exists to continue that ministry of reconciliation among men until the end of time and the gospel it has to preach is, as Pope Paul says in *Paenitemini*, a gospel of repentance. In somewhat similar terms the Order of Penance sets out the background for its consideration of the sacrament of reconciliation.

The material of the Introduction (1-2) can be summarised under seven heads:

1 The Father showed his love and mercy for mankind by reconciling the world to himself in Christ (II Cor. 5: 18 ff), making peace by the blood of the cross (Col. 1: 20) and delivering man from the slavery of sin.

2 This is why he began his earthly life by announcing a gospel of repentance: 'Repent and believe the gospel' (Mark 1: 4).

3 But he did not merely exhort people to repentance and urge them to abandon sin and turn with their whole hearts (*metanoia*) to God. He welcomed sinners and reconciled them with the Father (Luke 5: 20, 23; 7: 48). His healing of the sick was a sign of his power to remit sins and, we may add, a sign of his compassion for all who suffered whether in body or soul. The connection between bodily disease and sin, so prominent in the Old Testament, is present here too.[1]

4 But if his life was a ministry of reconciliation, it was by his passion, death and resurrection that he delivered mankind from sin: 'He died for our sins and rose again to make us righteous'

[1] See *Christian Celebration: the Sacraments*, p. 11.

(Rom. 4: 25). And so it was that 'on the night he was betrayed, he inaugurated his saving passion, instituted the sacrifice of the new covenant, made in his blood for the taking away of sins, and after his resurrection gave the Holy Spirit to the apostles that they might have the power to forgive or to retain sins. The same Spirit sent them to preach repentance and the remission of sins to mankind in the name of Christ.'

5 The church continues this mission and it was to Peter, who first responded in faith to his call, that Jesus said: 'I will give to you the keys of the kingdom of heaven and whatever you bind on earth, shall be bound in heaven and whatever you loose on earth, shall be loosed in heaven' (Matt. 16: 19). On the day of Pentecost, after proclaiming the passion, death and resurrection of Christ, he exhorted the people to repent and to be baptised in the name of Jesus Christ for the remission of their sins (Acts 2: 38). 'From that day onwards the church has never ceased to call men from sin to repentance (conversionem) and to proclaim Christ's victory over death by the celebration of penance.'

6 But, the Order notes, the first preaching about reconciliation was connected with baptism, in which the victory over death was manifested, through which unredeemed man could be crucified with Christ and the body of sin might be destroyed so that we should no longer be slaves of sin but, risen with Christ, we might live for God (Rom. 6: 4–10).

Further, the eucharist is the supreme sacrament-sign of God's reconciliation. In it the passion of Christ is made present (repraesentatur) and his body that was given up for us and his blood that was poured out for the taking away of sins are offered by the church to God for the salvation of the world. The Order refers to the third eucharistic prayer to emphasise this point: 'See the victim whose death has reconciled us to yourself', and concludes by recalling the words of eucharistic prayer II: 'may all of us who share the body and blood of Christ be brought together in unity by the Holy Spirit', for union with God is the end and purpose of reconciliation.

7 Finally, there is the sacrament of penance by which Christians who have fallen into sin after baptism may be restored to grace and reconciled with God. This is a ministry of the church and was committed by Christ to his apostles and their successors.

The line of thought is clear, moving from Christ who came to reconcile men to his Father through repentance, to the church which has the means of reconciliation in baptism, the eucharist and penance. In this perspective we can see that the *church* is the sacrament-sign of the ministry of forgiveness and reconciliation and that penance is in the here and now the sacrament of the forgiving and reconciling church. Like all the other sacraments, like the liturgy as a whole, the sacrament of penance manifests and makes present in the world now the redeeming power of Christ, the very heart of which is the paschal mystery. It is a particular example of the activity of Christ the priest in his church, and because 'Christ is always present in his church' reconciliation with the church signifies reconciliation with Christ.[1]

One consequence of this view is that since penance is the sacrament-sign of the reconciliation of Christ in the church it must have some elements of a public liturgy. The Order has done something to make this possible (48–59). It is one of the odder features of liturgical history that penance which was a very public liturgy indeed in the early centuries of the church's life has become entirely private. The penitent disappears into a 'box', which I do not think anyone has suggested might be a sacramental sign, the priest wears a stole which no one can see and during the words of absolution raises his hand which even the penitent usually cannot see. The medieval custom of confessing people in the chancel at least made the sacrament a *visible act*.[2]

Reconciliation in the Life of the Church (3–5)
Penance is an act of the church and the church is at once holy and yet always in need of purification.[3] The Constitution on the Liturgy (9) says that the church must always preach faith and penitence even to its own people. It must also 'prepare them for the sacraments (including therefore penance), teach them to observe all that Christ commanded and invite them to all the works of charity, piety and the apostolate. For all these works

[1] See CL 7, 2 and 41–2.
[2] 'Boxes' and grills date from the sixteenth century.
[3] The Order is quoting Vatican II, *De Ecclesia*, 8. The phrase is '*semper purificanda*' which comes close to '*semper reformanda*' and the two mean much the same thing. It reminds one of Luther's '*simul iustus et peccator*' which if separated from Luther's theology is true: we are 'justified' but always (repentant) sinners.

15

make clear that Christ's faithful, though not of the world, are to be the light of the world and to glorify the Father before men.'

The church is holy and therefore has within itself the sources of holiness—or rather these it receives from the Head who loved the church and gave himself up for it to sanctify it (Eph. 5: 25–26). But the members of the church are subject to temptation and often fall into sin; the church, united with Christ who himself was untouched by sin and came to atone for the sins of men, can receive sinners and dispense Christ's redeeming mercy.

This ministry of penitence is exercised in a great variety of ways in the life of the church. The Christian people, by accepting their sufferings, share in the passion of Christ. By doing works of mercy and charity and undergoing conversion day by day in response to the demands of the gospel they become a sign to the world of the need to turn to God. This same penitence is expressed and 'lived' in the liturgy where the people confess that they are sinners and implore the pardon both of God and of each other whether in penitential services, in the proclamation of God's word, or in the penitential rites of the eucharist. What the Order is saying is that the life of the whole church, both within the liturgy and outside it, is constantly constructing the sacrament-sign of the church as a repentant people, as the place of reconciliation and peace with God.

It is broad vision and we should do well to see things this way though we ruefully reflect that it is not always fulfilled in practice. There are those who think that the 'discipline' of penance is an easy way out of sin, and the intramural squabbles of the Catholic community hardly give the impression of a people who have attended to the apostolic injunction 'Be reconciled' (II Cor. 5: 20). But perhaps it is those 'works of mercy and charity', which translated into modern terms means service of the community, that we have been most deficient in. It becomes clear as one reflects on this Order that all the time it is striving to point people to think of others, of the church which, said St Ambrose, is wounded by our sins, and of the 'world' which, consciously or not, is awaiting a word and a credible example of a community that is both reconciled and by its every effort trying to reconcile man with man and man with God. Whatever is to be said of our achievement, it is the message of the Order that penance and the penitence that follows from it can never be complete unless and until it becomes concerned with human society.

Of this penitential life of the church the sacrament of penance

16

is a particular and particularly important sign. Of this two things may be said, one that is not mentioned by the Order and the other that is. The first is that penance is the actualisation of all the penitential activity of the church as a whole and of the individual Christian as such. The elements of this truth can be found in St Thomas, who saw the acts of the penitent—contrition, confession and satisfaction—as made effective by the absolution. Contrition, that in the nature of the case has to come before absolution, becomes effective of forgiveness and reconciliation through the action of Christ in the sacrament.[1] The basis of this view is that the church is itself the primary sacrament of Christ which is brought into action by the sacraments. But the church is *people* and it is their life of penitence and prayer as well as their sorrow and amendment of life that are actualised in the sacrament of penance.

The second truth that we find in the Order, one that has been a commonplace of theologians for the last twenty years, is that by penance we are reconciled both with God *and* the church which, as the text goes on quoting from Vatican II, we have wounded by our sins.[2] As has been observed often enough, penance has become the most individualistic of all sacraments. Liturgically, it has become a *tête-à-tête* with God; psychologically, it has not always been even that, for either the personality of the confessor or the obsession of the penitent with self has blocked out God. In any case, there was no sense that *my* sins had anything to do with the church and only rarely and in specific cases with other people. The Order clearly wishes to change this situation. In penance 'Christians obtain mercy from God whom they have offended and *at the same* time are reconciled to the church' (4). Again, the Order emphasises the solidarity of mankind in sin and also in holiness: 'By the mysterious dispensation of God men are linked by supernatural necessity to one another so that the sin of one injures another, just as the holiness of one is of benefit to another.' Penitence, then, carries with it reconciliation with members of the church whom we have injured by sin (5). The Order concludes by saying that, as sometimes people co-operate in sin, in the same way by repenting and doing penance they can help each other for, now delivered from sin by the grace of Christ, they can together

[1] See B. Poschmann, *Penance and the Anointing of the Sick* (Burns & Oates, 1964), pp. 168 ff.
[2] *Const. on Church*, 11 (Abott, p. 28). St Ambrose is particularly strong on this notion: 'It is the church that is wounded by our sins' (*De Virgin.* PL 16, c. 278).

and with all Christians work for justice and peace in the world (*ibid.*). This last phrase is perhaps the most significant in showing that the penitence of the individual and that of the church as a whole must be worked out in the affairs of the world.

There is another point that could well have received emphasis here though it is adequately expressed in the liturgy of penitential services later on. The church of the first five or six centuries was conscious of its solidarity in and through *prayer* and in few ecclesial actions was this so conspicuous as in penance. It was the prayer of the whole church that availed penitents and this was particularly evident in Lent (when it came to be fully organised) and in the 'prayers of the faithful' in which there was regularly prayer for sinners. In the mind of the early church it was prayer, both that of the people and of the bishops, that was the efficacious means by which sinners were reconciled to God and to the church. The evidence, which is abundant, can be seen as summed up in the phrase of St Leo: 'God's pardon can only be obtained by the supplications of bishops.'[1] It has even been said, with perhaps a touch of exaggeration, that the purpose of the penitential discipline was as much to incite the church to prayer for sinners as to secure the requisite amendment of life on the part of the sinners.[2]

This is all the more comprehensible if, with E. Schillebeeckx, we see that the church's prayer engages the intercession of the heavenly Christ (Heb. 5: 27): 'What Christ does invisibly as Lord (*Kyrios*) by his own glorified body, that he does in a visible way by his earthly body, the church, which indeed "prays and intercedes without cease for us". . . . In penance particularly which is the sacrament where we have lost the communal sense of the sacraments more than anywhere else, the grace of the remission of sins is assured to the penitent *because Christ prays with the church for the sinner*.'[3] We can add that it is Christ precisely as *priest* who makes intercessions for us and that 'the liturgy is an exercise of the priestly office of Jesus Christ'.[4] Here in this sacra-

---

[1] See B. Poschmann, *op. cit.*, p. 99: '*ut indulgentia Dei nisi supplicationibus sacerdotum nequeat obtineri*' (Eph. 18: 3). '*Sacerdos*' at this time usually meant 'bishop' and it was he who reconciled the sinner.

[2] A. G. Martinot, *L'Eglise en Prière* (Desclée, 1961), p. 573.

[3] E. H. Schillebeeckx, *Le Christ, sacrament de la rencontre de Dieu* (Editions du Cerf, 1960), pp. 99–100; Eng. trans. *Christ the Sacrament* (Sheed & Ward, 1963), Ch. II.

[4] CL 7.

ment he makes available to the sinner the forgiveness and reconciliation which he made possible by the cross. It is in this way that he acts in this sacrament and enables us to share in the mystery of his passion, death and resurrection. It is not for nothing that the early Fathers spoke of penance as a second baptism.[1]

Finally, as we know from the Gelasian Sacramentary, the solemn reconciliation of penitents on Maundy Thursday consisted solely of prayer. The deacon introduces the penitents with a long exhortation which is really a prayer and the bishop 'absolves', that is reconciles, them with a prayer.[2] It is, in the language of St Leo, the *supplicatio sacerdotis* by which sins are forgiven. As long as the 'absolution' was in the form of a prayer, it was easy to see that the sacrament engages the prayer of Christ. In the new Order, although the indicative formula of absolution has been retained, the first and longer part of the text is a prayer.

[1] It is also why they had for some time difficulty in accepting more than one remission of sins.

[2] See *Christian Celebration: the Sacraments*, pp. 214–15.

19

CHAPTER FOUR

The Sacrament of Penance and its Parts (6–7)

Under article **6** the Order describes the sacrament under four heads: contrition, confession, satisfaction and absolution. This pattern was formalised by the thirteenth-century Scholastics, notably St Thomas Aquinas, and was 'canonised' by the Council of Trent.[1] The first three are the 'acts of the penitent' and the fourth that of the priest and *together* they make up the sign of the sacrament though from the point of view of *sign* the acts of the penitent are the more important element.[2] This is true theologically, but liturgically speaking it has the immense advantage of showing that the penitent 'is not only the passive recipient of this grace but is the one who, together with the priest, actively celebrates the sacred *mysterium* itself which is the sacramental cause of the grace which he receives'.[3] This statement, though written before Vatican II, gives a description of penance as a liturgical celebration which is perfectly in accord with the *Constitution on the Liturgy* (7, 14). The acts of the penitent, prompted by the grace of God, become with the absolution the means of pardon and reconciliation.[4]

This is the positive value of this pattern and it is as well to recall these 'forgotten truths concerning penance'.[5] No doubt it was practically impossible for the revisers to take any other pattern, though it should be remembered that it is no older than the thirteenth century. It will be useful to recall briefly the older

[1] Denz. (17th ed.), 896–906.
[2] See K. Rahner, *Theological Investigations*, II (Darton, Longman & Todd, 1963), p. 156 and p. 159: in stating that the acts of the penitent are the 'matter' and the absolution the 'form' St Thomas is merely stating 'what had always been the conviction of the Fathers'.
[3] *Op. cit.*, p. 159.
[4] This is why Scotus's view that the acts of the penitent are only *conditiones sine quibus non* of pardon and the absolution the sole cause of pardon must be regarded as less than satisfactory.
[5] The title of Rahner's article, *op. cit.*, pp. 135 ff.

pattern. In the classical centuries of penance the sinner either submitted himself willingly to the bishop or was 'excommunicated'. That is, he was 'summoned' to take up the discipline of penance. If he was 'put under the ban', this was not intended as a penalty but rather as a means of pointing out that his situation was incompatible with the nature of the church, of which he was a member, and of calling him to the healing of pardon and reconciliation. Once he submitted himself to penance, he confessed his sin(s) privately to the bishop who administered the *correptio*, that is faced him with the demands of the gospel and encouraged him to take up the discipline of penance. Nor was this regarded as mere 'discipline'; it was part of the sacrament and was indeed the most visible part of the sacrament. Further, its main purpose was medicinal, to fit the penitent for the return to the full life of the church. The notion of punishment played but a small part in the whole affair. During this time the penitent profited from the prayer of the whole church and finally, often on Maundy Thursday, he was publicly reconciled ('absolved' in later terminology) by the prayer of the bishop.[1]

The order then here is: confession, penitence (satisfaction) and reconciliation which visibly was reconciliation with the church. The first was the response (prompted by grace) to the call of the church, in the person of the bishop, to repentance. Here was an authentic expression of the gospel command to preach repentance. The second was the response *in life* to the call and is much easier to understand than the performance of a 'penance' *after* reconciliation. The whole pattern is visibly liturgical, an act of the church understood both as the presiding clergy and as the whole people of God.[2]

Even when in the seventh and eighth centuries the Anglo-

[1] For the history of penance—a complicated matter—see B. Poschmann, *op. cit.*; P. M. Gy 'La Pénitence' in *L'Eglise en prière* (1961), pp. 569 ff; John Gunstone, *The Liturgy of Penance* (Faith Press, 1966).

[2] In his commentary in *Notitiae* already referred to, Sottocornola says that there is nothing to prevent satisfaction, which he prefers to call 'reparation', being performed in certain special cases *before* receiving 'the sign of reconciliation' (p. 68). He envisages this in certain cases laid down by the bishop for general or collective absolution. Since, however, this is something new for this generation, it will be necessary to consider it very carefully. Circumstances today do not ordinarily make it easy. However, it is interesting to observe that a writer nowadays can make this suggestion without any qualms if we remember the *furore* it created in seventeenth-century France when St Cyran and Antoine Arnauld suggested it.

Celtic practice of a more private form of penance was introduced into Europe much of the discipline, some of it very fierce (though mitigated by the dubious practice of 'redemptions')[1] remained, though reconciliation came after the penance. Understandably, some remained unreconciled until their death-beds and were then reconciled and anointed.[2] To this extent the ancient pattern was maintained. It is perhaps not insignificant that 'the first indulgences in the proper sense' appeared in eleventh-century France just at the time when penance was beginning to follow absolution.[3]

The Order now gives a summary description of the sacrament:

1 the penitent is moved by the Holy Spirit to penitence;
2 he must have a true contrition which carries with it confession, satisfaction and the intention to amend his life;
3 through the church God grants remission of sins which is effected (*operatur*) by the ministry of priests (**6**).

In this perspective it is possible to see that the four actions of penance are so many aspects of a whole through which Christ gives pardon and reconciliation. Contrition (normally) involves confession and confession is an expression of sorrow. Sorrow is taken up by the act of reconciliation. If the sacrament is to be fully understood it is necessary to keep all this in mind.

Contrition (6a)

Although contrition is described in the terms of the Council of Trent[4] its meaning is greatly deepened by relating it to the *metanoia* of the gospel. Quoting a key passage from *Paenitemini*, the Order[5] says that man can only approach the kingdom of Christ through *metanoia*, that is by a radical change of life. He reflects on his situation, he reviews his life and begins to put it in order and the motive for all this is the holiness and love of God which were shown forth in the Son and are abundantly communicated to us.[6] Obviously this is a pretty comprehensive account of contrition

---

[1] There was a tariff of penalties which, however, could be 'redeemed' by a more intensive form of penitence or even by getting other people to do it!

[2] See *Christian Celebration: the Sacraments*, p. 174.

[3] See K. Rahner, summarising Poschmann and Paulus, *op. cit.*, pp. 179–82. 'Indulgences in the proper sense succeeded to "absolutions" given as early as Gregory the Great which were *intercessions*.'

[4] Denz.-Schön. 1676 (ref. as given in *Ordo*).

[5] Eng. trans C.T.S., pp. 6–7.

[6] Heb. 1 : 2; Col. 1 : 19 and Eph. 1 : 23 are referred to: Christ is the fulness of the Godhead and through him comes reconciliation and peace.

and at once indicates the far-reaching demands of true repentance. If it were taken into account, it would transform our whole practice of the sacrament of penance. It might mean that fewer people went to confession simply because they could not meet the demands of repentance of this kind and the Order itself remarks that the genuineness of penance depends totally on conversion of heart.[1] But this doctrine also emphasises that a good deal of preaching and teaching will have to be done if people generally are to realise that this is what the sacrament of penance requires. This is one reason why services of penitence are necessary if people are to be confronted not with the 'rules' of the moral theology manuals but with the demands of the gospel.

Confession (6b)

From the time of Tertullian the avowal of faults was known as *exomologesis* which meant a great deal more than a detailing of sins. The word is a noun coming from the same verb used in some of the praising psalms (e.g. *Confitemini Domino*, 135). Confession was not merely a verbal admission of sin, it was an act of worship, a recognition of the reality of God and of what he demands of us. The text of the Order looks back rather to this tradition than to the more recent one: confession is at once the expression of what we *are* before God and of the contrition we have already conceived in our hearts. As we have suggested above, in confession is a mode of contrition, the humble avowal of faults before God, and if this is understood it follows that confession is not so much a strict accounting of sins but a placing of oneself before God as a sinner seeking his forgiveness. As in contrition so in confession, God is at the centre of the picture. If justification is sought for the audible confession of sins it is to be found along these lines rather than in the sphere of providing 'matter' for judgment.

Confession of sin is also of course part of the 'sacramentality' of penance. We can contemplate God in the secret places of our heart but we also need to express our prayer in words. We can, and must, conceive sorrow for sin in our hearts but we also feel

[1] This, however, does not mean that *confessors* should make exorbitant demands of the penitent either in the matter of 'perfect' contrition or in the matter of renewal of life ('penance'). What I mean is that when the penitent sees the full force of the sacrament he will perhaps hesitate before committing himself to its demands. He will begin to understand something of the magnitude of his sin and see that he must make real efforts to take his life in hand. But of course no one, however weak but of good will, should be repelled from the sacrament.

the need to express that sorrow in words. That is what 'confession' is and, as we have observed above, it is one of the means by which, with the priest, the penitent celebrates the sacrament. So the Order says that 'confession requires of the penitent the intention of opening his heart to God's minister' who represents the church.

As for the minister, he has to exercise a *'spirituale iudicium'* and I think the Order wishes to indicate that this is a very special kind of 'judgment'. The prominence of the Holy Spirit in the liturgy of this Order and the mention here of a 'spiritual judgment' incline one to think that what is meant comes nearer to the 'discernment of spirits' which in the recent past has been too restricted in its connotation. Quite apart from the question of spiritual counsel, the Order seems to be saying that the confessor must be able to read the soul of the penitent. He must at least understand and seek to discern his condition.[1] No doubt this view makes great demands of the confessor, but it is important and puts the judgment aspect of the sacrament in a very different light.

The Order goes on to say that the confessor exercises this power of judgment acting 'in the person of Christ' and gives sentence which remits or retains sins by the power of the keys.[2] This last part of the phrase comes from the Council of Trent (Cap. 5) though we note that later (Cap. 6) the judgment is described as *'ad instar actus iudicialis'*, that is, 'after the manner of a judicial act'. In the past, since the Council of Trent, a great deal has been made of the judicial nature of penance and perhaps theologians have not been careful enough to note that even Trent uses secular judicial procedures as an *analogy*. More recently, an examination of the matter has shown that the differences between a secular act of judgment and that of penance are considerable. A good deal of dubious exegesis, especially of John 20: 22, 23, has sought to 'prove' that a judicial act on the lines

[1] I am led to think this way because Père Ligier, who was a member of the first group for the reform of penance, has observations bearing on this matter in LMD (1967, 90) where he considers the eastern tradition of penance. Thus he writes in one place (p. 161): 'In the eastern perspective the administration of this sacrament requires not simply the *power* of the Holy Spirit but also a familiarity with the divine things which is possessed by those who live in the Spirit and know the things of God and the secrets of hearts' [emphasis ours]. He refers to Origen *De Oratione*, 28. The confessor in the eastern tradition is the 'holy man'. The whole article seems to have influenced the redaction of the Order.

[2] Matt. 16: 19; 18: 18; John 20: 22, 23.

of a secular judgment was part of its meaning. But from the beginning the church has 'bound' only that she may loose: 'Binding and loosing are not two sides of an alternative, but two phases of the one reaction whereby the Holy Church answers the sins of one of her members.'[1] The purpose of the binding is to uncover the anomalous situation of the sinner *vis-à-vis* the church which is holy and of which he is an unholy member. His belonging to the church is a contradiction of her holiness and 'this has to be brought to light on the visible plane of the church' and only then 'can the guilt towards the church and God be lifted or "loosed" again on the same plane, i.e. on the sacramental plane'. As Rahner goes on to say, this is how the early church always understood the matter. The 'binding' is essentially an act of mercy and not a condemnation with punishment attached.

To put the matter in another way, the priest in the confessional is not a (continental) judge seeking to reconstruct a crime in all its details so that he may meet out condign punishment. For one thing, the penitent is not capable of doing so. He would need an advocate not only to defend him but to put his case. With penance we have to do with a sacrament through which is dispensed the mercy of God and a sacrament is in the category of sign (*in genere signi*). The confession of the penitent is much more a sign of his repentance than a piece of criminal accounting. In practice, the penitent often confesses more than he expresses in words and, on the other hand, sometimes and unwittingly less. As for the priest's judgment, 'his human meeting with this sinfulness, is only (again) a *sign*—often a very imperfect and shadowy sign—of the merciful salvific judgment of God.[2] The priest is the *minister* (servant) of Christ, not his substitute.

Again, confession is self-accusation. The penitent wishes to make himself 'a beggar before God', displaying all his wretchedness, his weaknesses and his sins. It is at this point that the notion of confession as a mode of repentance becomes important. The difference between this procedure and that of the secular courts hardly needs to be pointed out. It must of course be added that the

[1] Rahner, *op. cit.*, p. 142.

[2] For the foregoing see L. Monden, *Sin, Liberty and Law* (Geoffrey Chapman, 1966), p. 47. The author goes on to say that both priest and penitent may be wrong in their judgment and they often are, more often than is supposed, but this does not matter for if both are in good faith 'God forgives not what has been confessed but what has been signified by the confession'. This is sound sense and, if known, would have saved many from scruples.

confessor needs to know the condition of the penitent for first, penance is a sacrament which of its nature demands an expression of sin and, secondly, it is only if the confessor knows the condition of the penitent that he will be able to help him to begin to live again as a full and healthy member of the church.

Once this is understood, it is possible to see that, as the Council of Trent taught, the priest's judgment and subsequent absolution are not mere declarations that the sinner is free from sin but that *both* are sacramental. Penance is a sacrament of this sort. The priest is not there *in propria persona*, but, precisely as the Order says, *in persona Christi*, and that means that he must try to bring to his task something of the understanding and compassion of Christ.

Satisfaction (6c)

This is the most difficult and contentious part of penance and both 'Protestants and Eastern Christians' object to 'the Catholic teaching on punishment due to sin, satisfaction and indulgences'.[1] In practice and in spite of what has been written and said for years on the subject, it is the most devalued part of the sacrament. Great numbers of people feel that 'saying your penance' is too easy even if it be said that it is 'the sacramental penance', i.e. part of the sacrament.

We can be thankful then that the Order is both reserved and positive on the subject. It nowhere uses the sacred phrase 'temporal punishment due to sin' and is content to speak of 'reparation for the damage caused by sin' of 'the order injured by sin' and of the 'disease' (*morbo*) which is 'to be cured by the appropriate remedy'. The Order speaks of 'restoration', 'cure' and 'renewal of life', all of which it sees as the positive values of penance in the stricter sense. There is no suggestion of legalism

---

[1] K. Rahner, *op. cit.*, pp. 194–5. He writes in the same place: 'Only a more profound doctrine about temporal punishment can offer any prospect of our being able to break down the objections of the Protestants and Eastern Christians.' One difficulty I have is that I cannot find any basis for the distinction between sin and the 'punishment due to sin' in the New Testament. When God forgives, he forgives all. The difficulty comes partly from the postponement of satisfaction until after absolution. Although it would perhaps be an over-simplification to say that the Fathers regarded satisfaction as medicinal and as concerning the church (and of course the penitent) rather than God, that is the impression one carries away from them. As, however, Rahner remarks, this does not mean that there could not have been a developing insight in the matter.

here. In the last sentence there is one phrase that seems to be of great significance and it is surprising that it has not appeared earlier: the penitent forgetting those things that are behind (Phil. 3:13) and extending his vision to the future 'inserts himself anew into the mystery of salvation' through the practice of penitence which now becomes the programme of his whole life.

Turning the phrase a little differently,[1] we may say that 're-insertion' into the mystery of salvation, that is into the passion, death and resurrection of Christ, is of the very essence of the sacrament. We naturally think of the 'insertion' of the individual into the mystery of Christ first through baptism and then through the eucharist. But if Christ came to take away 'the sin of the world' (John 1:29), it is here in penance that in a special way this happens. The sinner meets the saving, forgiving Christ with whom he is reconciled so that once again he may take up the 'following of Christ' which means sharing in his passion and death that he may come to resurrection.

In this perspective 'penance' in the stricter sense, but also in a much deeper sense than is customary, is the bridge between the celebration of the sacrament and the living of the Christian life in the world. This is the concern of the pope in *Paenitemini*:[2] 'Following the Master, every Christian must renounce himself, take up his cross, and participate in the sufferings of Christ. Thus transformed into the image of Christ's death, he is capable of meditating on the glory of the resurrection. Furthermore, following the Master, he can no longer live for himself but must live for him who loves him and gave himself for him. He will have to live for his brethren. . . .'[3] 'Living for the brethren'

---

[1] '*se inserit*' is better translated by a passive 'is inserted' for it is Christ in his church who makes the 'insertion', in this case the 're-insertion'.

[2] *Ed. and trans. cit.*, p. 7.

[3] A number of scripture references are given: Phil, 3:10–11; Rom. 6: 10; Gal. 2: 20; and finally Col. 1:24. The exegesis of this last text presents some difficulty. It hardly means what it is thought to mean in ascetical writing. '[The] completion of the sufferings of Christ is intimately connected with the completion of *the preaching of the gospel*. . . .' The 'sufferings of Christ' would then be the apostolic sufferings endured as the gospel is continually brought to new places until a certain quota is reached; see *The Jerome Biblical Commentary* (Geoffrey Chapman, 1966), *in loc.*, p. 338. See also J. H. Houlden, *Paul's Letters from Prison* (Pelican N.T. Commentaries, 1970), pp. 176–8, who points out that for Paul the Gospel = Christ. The best texts to use are first, the well-known one, Rom. 6: 10, and secondly, Phil. 3: 10–11: 'All I want is to know Christ and the power of his resurrection and to share his sufferings by reproducing the pattern of his death. . . .'

obviously means serving the brethren, so penitence in modern terms involves the whole of human life and this emphasis too is found in *Paenitemini*: '[The church] insists that the virtue of penance be exercised in persevering faithfulness to the duties of one's state of life, in the acceptance of the difficulties arising from one's work and from human coexistence, in the patient bearing of the trials of earthly life and of the utter insincerity that pervades it.'[1]

With this personal acceptance of the duties of one's state of life goes the obligation of service, which is expressed in the terms of 'works of mercy or charity'. We may no longer like this terminology. It has been associated with a spirituality that was both inward-looking (you 'did good' to others to 'gain merit' or to do good ultimately to yourself) and somewhat patronising. Christians of today have gone far beyond these notions and it is the concept of service that predominates. Perhaps now there needs to be a clearer realisation that service is difficult, that, in Baron von Hügel's phrase, it is 'costing', and that the very sufferings and disappointments it brings are a sharing in the sufferings of Christ.

So there *is* a satisfactory theology of penitence but at this point we are moved to expostulate: 'That is all very well. But what has this got to do with the sacrament of penance as it is now used?' This has been one of the complaints of the young about penance[2] who *are* willing to take up various forms of service for the community. The saying of Five Hail Marys does not appeal to them at all. It is here that public services of penitence can perform an important role. While urging other aspects of their use, the Order (25 and 37, less strongly) recommends that such services should be used to 'promote works of charity towards God and our neighbour'. We shall return to the matter.

Absolution (6d)

Faithful to the sacramental theology of the *Constitution on the Liturgy* (7), the revisers describe absolution as 'the sign by which God grants pardon' and conclude 'thus the sacrament is completed'. To make no mistake about this they continue: 'By the divine economy, as God willed that the kindness and love [*phi-*

---

[1] *Ed. and trans. cit.*, p. 9, III, A, and see B for other kinds of imposed sufferings.
[2] See Mary Hallaway in *Penance: Virtue and Sacrament*, pp. 9 ff, and *Christian Celebration: the Sacraments*, p. 220.

lanthropia in the Greek] of God our Saviour appeared visibly to mankind (Tit. 3: 4–5), so it was his will to grant us salvation by visible signs and to renew the covenant broken' by sin. This at once removes any legalist suggestion from absolution and puts the whole sacrament in the context of the history of salvation which reached its culmination in the incarnation of the Son of God (CL 5).

This impression is reinforced by the following passage, which draws heavily on the parable of the prodigal son (Luke 15: 11–24). The whole passage is worth giving:

> 'By the sacrament of penance therefore the Father welcomes the repentant son who comes back to him, Christ puts the lost sheep on his shoulder and brings him back to the fold and the Holy Spirit sanctifies once more the one who is the temple of the Spirit. . . . Finally, all this is manifested (one might almost translate, 'celebrated') through a renewed or more fervent participation in the table of the Lord's eucharist in which, now that the son has returned from a distant land, there is great joy in the banquet of the church of God.'

This passage perhaps more than any other in the Order gives the church's view of the meaning of penance. There is the saving mercy of God, Father, Son and Holy Spirit, who are each active in the return of the sinner, and the eucharist is revealed as the culmination of the process of pardon and reconciliation, as it is the culmination of all the sacraments. The way to it has been barred by sin but now that the barrier is removed, pardon and reconciliation are achieved by encounter with the redeeming Christ.

The Necessity and Usefulness of Penance

The sacrament is *necessary* for the reconciliation of those who have cut themselves off from the love of God by grave sin and it is *useful* to those who fall into lesser, 'venial', sins and who wish to strengthen themselves so that they may live more fully as the free children of God. We note here how sin is described: it is a recession from communion with God of which the bond is love (*recesserunt . . . a communione caritatis Dei*). Sin, in other words, is a breaking of loving union with God, which comes to a great deal more than the infringement of a legal code.

While the Order repeats the injunction of the Council of Trent about the confession of sins (**7b**), it does so without any special emphasis on the matter: each and every mortal sin of which the penitent is conscious must be confessed. No doubt there is no discussion here because it is the received doctrine of the church and, since the Council of Trent came to no definitive solution of whether this was a matter of divine or ecclesiastical law, the revisers wished to leave the matter alone. It has some relevance, however, to the General Absolution of sins and we will say a word about it there.

The statement on the usefulness of confessing venial sins is more remarkable. It puts the whole matter in the context of the Christian *life*. Such confessions are not 'merely ritualistic repetitions nor some sort of psychological exercise' but a continued effort (*studium*) to perfect *the grace of baptism*. In other words, the sacrament used in this way is an effort to live out the implications of baptism in which we were first made like Christ and received our calling to suffer with him that we may rise to a new life with him. The Order goes on: 'we bear in our bodies the death of Jesus Christ so that his life may be ever more clearly manifested in us' (II Cor. 4: 10). The whole purpose of such confession is that we should become more like Christ in the depths of our being and more attentive to the voice of the Spirit.

This, I think, is a much more profound view of confessions of venial sin than has ever been given before. Confession is seen as a continuing means of living the life of penitence that is incumbent on every Christian. What the church is saying is that since repentance, pardon and reconciliation are part of the life of the sinner which is actualised and culminates in the sacrament of penance, so also 'confessions of devotion' (a term that is avoided), if put into the total context of the evangelical life, are part of the 'following of Christ'. Provided, in other words, they are not 'ritualistic exercises' which do not engage the life of the penitent, such confessions will naturally form part of the practice of every serious Christian.

However, as we have recalled above, 'if this sacrament is to have its full force in the life of the Christian it is necessary that it should reach right down to the roots of his life and move him (*impellat*) to a more fervent service of others' (**7b**).

This section closes with a comprehensive description of the sacrament: 'The celebration of this sacrament is always an action of the Church in which it proclaims its faith, gives thanks to God

30

for the freedom with which Christ has made us free and offers its life as a spiritual sacrifice to the praise of the glory of God while hastening to the (final) encounter with Christ.' The first point—that penance is an action of the church—emphasises its ecclesial character: we are reconciled to God and the church and the latter as the body of Christ makes its contribution to the reconciliation of sinners. The proclamation of faith, which according to the Constitution is an essential requirement of sacramental celebration, is, as we shall see, effected even in private use of the sacrament by an announcement of God's word. But it should also be emphasised that it is a proclamation of faith in the forgiving, reconciling Christ. He is not just a generalised figure.

What is more surprising is that the revisers have determinedly shown that the sacrament of penance is *an act of worship*: through its celebration, in whatever form, it is a recognition of the glory of God, an act of thanksgiving and an offering of the Christian's life. This thought establishes another link with the eucharist and is a matter that might well be pursued in greater depth. The final phrase emphasises the eschatological dimension of penance as the new Orders do for all the sacraments. The conclusion must be that penance, like all the sacraments and indeed the whole liturgy, is part of the on-going life of the Christian which is to be seen in the context of the history of salvation reaching from creation in the beginning to the second coming of Christ at the end. At the level of practice, it must be said that a great deal remains to be done to bring these notions into the forefront of people's thinking on this sacrament. The narrow, almost clinical character of the sacrament must give way to a richer and much more fruitful understanding which should do much to bring people back to celebrating it.

CHAPTER FIVE

The Use of the Sacrament (8–14)

Even here, in what is substantially a practical section, the Order betrays theological depth and what one can only call pastoral compassion.

'The whole church as the priestly people' is involved in different ways in the ministry of reconciliation. The church by preaching calls sinners to repentance but also prays for them and with a motherly care and concern comes to their aid, encouraging them to acknowledge and confess their sins so that they may obtain the saving mercy of God.

How this is to be done in practice is another matter. We are even a little hesitant about praying for a category called 'sinners' when we are conscious, more so than perhaps in the past, that we are all sinners. But at any rate in Lent it should be possible to include discreetly worded petitions in the intercessions of the Mass and, if the ministry of the laity in this matter must be a very delicate one, there is no doubt that 'care and concern' shown by members of the Christian community for those who are either temporarily or, as it would seem, permanently outside it can do much to keep them attached to the church. Here again there is a case for re-thinking our pastoral methods and policy.

The principal ministry of conversion and absolution is of course that entrusted by Christ to his apostles and their successors, namely bishops and priests 'who act in communion with the bishops and by his authority'. They perform this ministry not merely by 'hearing confessions' but by preaching the gospel of repentance and calling people to conversion of life. In the celebration of penance, however done, 'in the name of Christ and by the power of the Holy Spirit they bear witness to the remission of sins and impart it'. The constant recalling in this Order of the operation of the Holy Spirit is very remarkable. It was a feature very prominent in the thinking and practice of the early church and the laying-on of hands (of which a vestige still remains) was

32

the symbol of this communication of the Holy Spirit in the reconciliation of the sinner to the church. Here as in the formula of
absolution (46) our minds are carried back to the giving of the
Spirit to the Apostles and their commissioning to forgive sins
(John 20: 22–23).

The Confessor

Against this background the qualities and function of the confessor are described. He is to have the necessary knowledge and
prudence which he will acquire by the necessary study and use
his knowledge 'under the guidance of the church'. He must
pray for guidance. With this equipment he should be able to
discern the illnesses of the soul, provide apt remedies and 'wisely
exercise the function of judge'. Here the Order is explicit: judgment is an exercise of the 'discernment of spirits which is a gift
of the Holy Spirit, giving an intimate knowledge of the workings
of God in the human heart'. It is perhaps a surprising addition
though a valuable one. 'Discernment of spirits' has usually been
thought of as the gift of special people who can guide those in the
higher reaches of the spiritual life—or alternatively those who
could discern diabolical from benign spirits at work in the heart.
If then the ordinary confessor is exercising 'discernment of spirits'
the need to pray that he may be rightly guided is all the more
urgent.

The Order sees the confessor as performing a fatherly function—a notion that is wholly traditional (cf. the old song 'My
ghostly fader') bearing in himself the image of Christ and revealing
to the penitent whom he welcomes 'the heart of the Father'. The
confessor is then a sign in himself, a sign of the Father's love
shown forth in the Son. By consequence, he is exercising a
function of Christ himself 'who in mercy effected the work of
redemption and who by his power is present in the sacraments'.[1]

This must be said to be a 'high' doctrine of the role of the
confessor. If, as the Order indicates, the acts of the penitent are
part of the sacrament, the same is evidently true of the role of
the confessor and as in the Mass he is the sacrament-sign of
Christ, so is he here. But as in the Mass the priests can become
an opaque sign, this is also possible in the sacrament of penance.
The more exact parallel is with the priest as minister of the word
in the eucharist when he is conscious that his own personality

[1] A reference is given to CL 7.

and his defects can obscure the image of Christ. The consequence must be that the confessor must prepare himself for his task with great seriousness and in the exercise of his function, it is clear from the Order, he must make present the mercy of the Father and the compassion of Jesus Christ. This is the spirit not merely of this section but of the whole Order. Harshness, rebuke, inquisitorial questionings and censoriousness are out of harmony with it.

The Penitent

Here the Order is brief, first because it has already dealt with the acts of the penitent (**6 a, b, c**) and secondly because it has something to say about the matter from a practical point of view lower down (**17–20**). The Order is content to emphasise what is undoubtedly the important truth that through his acts (repentance, confession and satisfaction) the sinner is playing his (necessary) part in the celebration of the sacrament: 'Thus the Christian, while experiencing God's mercy and proclaiming it by his life, celebrates with the priest the liturgy of the church which continually renews itself' (**11**).

Of the Ministers and their Functions: The Celebration of Penance

In this section certain practical directives are to be found:
1 Except in danger of death only those priests with canonical 'faculties' may exercise the ministry of sacramental penance (**9b**).
2 The *place* of penance remains what it is in current canon law (CIC 909) but conferences of bishops may arrange otherwise.[1]
3 The confessor must always carefully keep 'the seal of confession'.
4 Priests must be willing to hear people's confessions whenever they reasonably ask and 'although the reconciliation of penitents may be celebrated at any hour or on any day', fixed times should be made known to the people. This is regularly done, though perhaps we might be more flexible about them. Saturday evenings are proving to be one of the worst times for confession.
5 Lent is a particularly favourable time for the celebration of the sacrament of penance for 'on Ash Wednesday the people hear the call "repent and believe the gospel"'. Communal services of penance should take place at this time and opportunities

[1]See p. 84.

should be given to all the faithful 'to be reconciled with God and their neighbour' so that, spiritually renewed, they may celebrate the paschal mystery at the end of Lent. This is but one of the many touches that relates the sacrament of penance to the paschal mystery. Like the Mass, like all the other sacraments, penance is a celebration of the paschal mystery through which and by the power of Christ we die to self and are raised up to a new kind of life.

We shall have to refer to these matters again in a more pastoral context.

CHAPTER SIX

The Reconciliation of Individual Penitents
(41–47)

The rite for the reconciliation of individual penitents is first described in the Introduction (15–20) and its texts given in the first chapter (41–47). We will take the latter first.

1 The confessor greets the penitent in a kindly manner and the penitent (and the priest if he wishes) makes the sign of the cross.

2 The confessor will then address the penitent in these or similar words: 'May God who has shed his light in our hearts give you the grace sincerely to recognise your sins and to acknowledge his mercy.'[1]

3 The confessor then reads a text of holy scripture from the selection provided (72–84). He may, however, omit this.

4 The penitent confesses his sins and listens to the counsel of the confessor 'who will exhort him to repent of his sins and remind him that the sacrament gives him the ability to die and rise with Christ and so to be renewed by the paschal mystery'. The confessor imposes the penance in 'satisfaction of the sins committed and to help in the amendment of the penitent's life'.

5 The confessor invites the penitent 'to manifest his sorrow' by a prayer of repentance for which various texts are provided (45, 85–92).

6 With his hands raised over the penitent (or at least his right hand) he pronounces the words of absolution which are as follows:

'God, Father of mercy,
reconciled the world to himself

---

[1] *Deus, qui illuxit in cordibus nostris det tibi ut in veritate agnoscas peccata tua et suam misericordian.* Another verb before 'misericordian' would have made translation easier. However, according to 42 it may in any case be adapted.

by the death and resurrection of his Son
and sent out the Holy Spirit to take away sins.
May he grant you pardon and peace through the ministry
of the church:
(And) I absolve you from your sins
in the name of the Father, Son and Holy Spirit'.

Resp. Amen[1]

7 After the absolution there is a brief 'thanksgiving': 'Let us
give thanks to the Lord for he is good'; and the penitent replies:
'For his love endures for ever' (Ps. 135). Finally, there is a
dismissal: 'The Lord has forgiven your sins. Go in peace.'[2]

Commentary

This rite, simple as it is, conforms to the now familiar pattern
of all the revised sacramental liturgies. There is the welcome of the
penitent, the proclamation of God's word, brief as it may be, the
'celebration of the sacrament' and the conclusion with its dismissal.

The Order (15–20) provides some commentary on the rite
and this we will now follow.
a The purpose of the phrase 'May God who has shed his light . . .'
or its equivalent is to stimulate the penitent's trust in God and
his goodness. The directive that follows gives support to the
practice, apparently on the increase, that sees confession as
something of a dialogue rather than the detailing of a list of sins.
The penitent is encouraged to make known to the confessor the
conditions of his life, what difficulties he finds in leading the
Christian life 'and whatever may be useful for the confessor to
know for the exercise of his ministry' (16). This is not laid down
as an obligation and it is for the penitent to take the initiative
in the matter. However, the confessor will *help* the penitent to
make an integral confession (18), though as the Order suggests

[1] *Deus, Pater misericordiarum,*
qui per mortem et resurrectionem Filii sui
mundum sibi reconciliavit
et Spiritum Sanctum effudit in remissionem peccatorum,
per ministerium Ecclesiae
indulgentiam tibi tribuat et pacem.
Et ego te absolvo a peccatis tuis
in nomine Patris et Filii et Spiritus Sancti.
[2] Other texts to be used at choice 1, no. 93.

(**10a**), this is not to be thought of as an inquisitorial procedure. As we know, the common teaching of the theologians is that the obligation of integrity rests on the penitent.

b The reading of the text of scripture which may be done either by the confessor or the penitent is a proclamation of faith which should help the penitent to discern his sinful condition and call him to repentance (**17**). It is an application of the rule that we are saved by faith, which comes from hearing, and the sacraments of faith.

In practice, it will no doubt be the priest who usually reads the text though it is clear that well thought out booklets for the people which shall be freely available are a requirement of a satisfactory celebration of penance. They will need to be a good deal fuller than the meagre formulas to be found in existing books—or in books that existed until recently. Most people nowadays do not use one at all.

c As well as helping the penitent to make his confession, the confessor will exhort him to repentance and provide appropriate counsel for the living of the Christian life. If necessary, he will instruct the penitent in the duties of the Christian life. In the case of damage, whether material (theft) or spiritual (e.g. calumny), he will 'lead the penitent to make fitting restitution'. Finally he will impose the 'penance' which is to be thought of not merely as expiation for past sins but as a remedy for weakness and help towards amendment of life. This may consist of prayers, self-denial but especially 'service of neighbour and works of mercy which will throw light on the *social nature of sin and its remission*'. Evidently, then, 'penances' that go far beyond prayers are envisaged and this is, as we have observed, one of the things that the young especially have looked for.[1]

The whole of this matter is put even more pregnantly in a rubric of this rite. After doing what has been set out above, the priest is instructed to recall to the penitent that 'the sacrament of penance gives him the ability to die with Christ and to rise again with him and so to be renewed by the paschal mystery' (**44**). The continued emphasis of the Order on penance as a celebration of and participation in the passion and resurrection of Christ is remarkable and certainly not fortuitous.

d Of the 'act of contrition' the Order says that as far as possible it should be a prayer made up of words from holy scripture (**19**). The text given under **45** hardly conforms to this requirement. Here is a rough translation:

[1]See p. 28

38

'My God, I repent with all my heart and I am sorry for all the wrong I have done and the good I have failed to do, because by my sins I have offended you, who are the supreme good, and more to be loved than anything else. With the help of your grace I am resolved to do penance, to sin no more and to avoid the occasions of sin. Through the merits of the passion of our Saviour Jesus Christ, have mercy on me, Lord.'

There are echoes here of formulas with which we are familiar and it must be said to be inclusive but it can hardly be said to reflect scriptural language.

The alternatives to be found later on (85–92) are much better. The first two consist of phrases from Psalms 24 and 50 and the third is taken verbatim from the gospel: 'Father, I have sinned against you; I am not worthy to be called your son. Be merciful to me, a sinner' (Luke 15: 18; 18: 13). The fourth is notable for its invocation of Father, Son and Holy Spirit:

'Father of mercy, as a repentant son I turn back to you and say: "I have sinned against you and am no longer worthy to be called your son. Jesus Christ, Saviour of the world, like the thief to whom you opened the gates of Paradise, I make my petition to you:
"Remember me, Lord, when you come into your kingdom.
Holy Spirit, source of love,
with all my trust I call upon you:
"Purify me. Give me the grace to walk as a child of light."'

The scriptural references are obvious.

A particular feature of the fifth formula is that it looks out to the church and the world:

'Lord Jesus,
you opened the eyes of the blind, healed the sick, forgave the woman who was a sinner
and after his fall you confirmed Peter in your love.
Receive my prayer. Free me from all my sins. Renew your love within me and give me the grace to live in perfect unity with the brethren and to proclaim your salvation to mankind.'

The shortest is simply: 'Lord Jesus, Son of God, have mercy on me, a sinner'—more or less Luke 18: 13.

All these forms of prayer are good and it is to be hoped that when booklets are prepared for the people they will be included. The tired formulas that are still current say very little to anyone and these new ones will stimulate people to true repentance.

e Of the old formula of absolution the first sentence: '*Dominus noster Jesus Christus te absolvat*' dates from the time (before the twelfth century) when absolution/reconciliation was given in the form of a prayer. This has now gone and is replaced by another, longer, formula which, as is clear from the Latin, is a *prayer* (*Deus . . . tribuat et pacem*). Although it is on the long side, it is a pity that the mediation of Christ in the action of forgiveness was not expressed. In the last analysis it is *Christ* who forgives even if 'through the ministry of the church'. The indicative form of absolution, which appeared in the twelfth century, has been retained and we rejoice that the heavy and for the most part irrelevant jargon of the old form has gone. Apart from this the formula seems to be new.

As with other new sacramental formulas there are here also unmistakable references to the New Testament. God in Christ reconciled the world to himself (II Cor. 5: 19) through the death and resurrection of his Son (see Rom. 8: 34, etc.) and he sent out the Holy Spirit for the taking away of sins (John 20: 22–23; and Acts 2: 1–11; 37–41). 'The ministry of the church' is included not merely to emphasise that the confessor is its representative but to remind us that reconciliation is an action of the church effected by the death and resurrection of Christ. So the Introduction: 'The formula of absolution shows that the reconciliation of the penitent proceeds from the mercy of the Father and indicates the link between reconciliation and the paschal mystery. The formula points up the role of the Holy Spirit in the taking away of sins and finally it reveals the ecclesial dimension of the sacrament for reconciliation with God is sought and given by the ministry of the church' (**19**).

Of the conclusion of the rite little needs to be said. A form of thanksgiving is obviously in place and there has to be a dismissal. But a brief look at other forms of conclusion is worth while (**93**). It is interesting to note that the first is the well-known one: 'May the passion of our Lord Jesus, the merits of the Blessed Virgin Mary and of all the saints, and whatever good you do, whatever sufferings you experience be *a remedy of your sins*, bring increase of grace and the reward of eternal life.' As is well known, St Thomas Aquinas and some others after him attributed considerable importance to this text which in the former rite always concluded the absolution. For him it had a peculiar efficacy as part of the sacrament. Speaking of the appropriateness of the confessor imposing a penance he writes: 'It is better that he should do so and at the same time make the penance something that is within the capacity of the penitent, through which he will in fact make satisfaction, rather than that he should impose one that would discourage him. At the same time he encourages him to take on greater-penances which have all the greater power to expiate his sins through the words of the priest: "whatever good you do, may bring about the remission of your sins".'[1] There will be some of other traditions than our own who do not care for this formula with its juxtaposition of 'the passion of our Lord Jesus Christ' and 'merits of the Blessed Virgin Mary and the saints' but the prayer expresses the whole economy of the body of Christ in which there is mutal aid of prayer and well-doing which constantly interact among the members of the body.[2] What makes the prayer more acceptable is that the phrase of the older text *in remissionem peccatorum* (for the taking away of sins) has been replaced with *in remedium peccatorum* (for a remedy of sin) which supports the interpretation I have suggested. It is the whole burden of the New Testament that because we are 'members one of another' we can help each other at the deepest level of the Christian life.[3]

Of the other three formulas the third is the most interesting. It reminds the penitent of the social dimension of penance: 'Go in peace and proclaim to the world the saving deeds of God who has saved you.'

[1] *Quodlibet*, III, 28 (Ed. Mandonnet, 1926, p. 125). And cf. K. Rahner who refers to this text though is dubious about Aquinas's view: *Op. cit.*, p. 173 n. 56. He also points out that the formula was 'quite new' in the thirteenth century.

[2] See OP 5 considered above.

[3] 'Merits' of course, if of Mary, the saints and ourselves are on an entirely different footing from those of Christ and are not merely worthless without his but impossible.

CHAPTER SEVEN

The Reconciliation of Several Penitents with Individual Absolution (48–59)

The Order has met in part the often-repeated request for a public liturgy of penance by providing a form which consists of a public ministry of the word and private absolution.

The case for a more public form of penance can be summed up like this:

1 All sacramental celebrations, by the terms of the Constitution on the Liturgy, demand a proclamation of God's word.

2 For penance it is particularly important that we should hear the urgent message of the Bible to repent.

3 The Order itself recognises that penance is an ecclesial and communal sacrament, that sin has effects on the community and that the sinner's reparation must be assisted by the community.

4 We sin not simply as individuals but as a community and some expression of that common sin is demanded by the nature of the case.

5 Prayer once formed a very important element of the sacrament and the Order recognises this. Common *prayer* for our own sins and those of others is thus made possible.

6 We need to be confronted with the demands of the gospel to live as followers of Christ and what is traditionally called 'examination of conscience' will be greatly more effective and searching if at least from time to time people are helped to make a more rigorous examination, to review their whole lives under the light of the gospel.

7 Psychologically this will be of particular assistance to those who find it difficult to reflect on themselves and consequently to confess their sins in the confessional.

8 While as we have seen there is a theological justification for 'making satisfaction', as it is at present practised it is unacceptable

to a great number of people who require something more realistic. This could be achieved if common tasks to be performed by members of the community were appointed as a 'visible' penance.[1]

The liturgy of the Order (22–30) has gone some way towards meeting these needs.

The Rite

1 The rite begins with a chant, a greeting, a brief address to the congregation and a collect.
2 The service of God's word follows.
3 The Homily.
4 Examination of conscience.
5 The General Confession (as in Penitential Rite I of the Order of Mass).
6 Prayer in a litanic form with the Lord's prayer.
7 Private confession and absolution.
8 Thanksgiving, blessing and dismissal.

Commentary

As will be seen, the pattern of the service is the now conventional one and does not call for extended treatment. A few points may be noted.

The service begins with the hearing of God's word, because God makes known his call to repentance and sorrow for sin by his word. The service, then, is the continued proclamation of the gospel message of repentance and since God is present in the scriptures when they are read out in church (CL 7), we can be sure that it is *his* call we are hearing (OP 24). There may be one or several readings which should be followed by psalms, other chants or silence so that the participants may come to 'a deeper understanding of God's word and assent to it in their hearts' (*ibid.*).

For this service first two models are given though a long list of further texts is given (101–201). Together they cover all the important texts of the Bible on sin, repentance, reconciliation and amendment of life. Commentary on all of them would take up a great deal of space and it is to be hoped that when booklets for the people are prepared a generous provision will be offered to

[1] This is a summary of what I have written in *Christian Celebration: the Sacraments*, pp. 213–21.

them. If one thing is clear about this Order it is that it provides a very rich anthology of scripture passages, psalms and prayers which could transform people's understanding and practice of the sacrament of penance. Here without any doubt is to be found the authentic teaching of the church on repentance and reconciliation.

The first model uses parts of Deut. 5 (substantially the Ten Commandments with the omission of sundry verses) and Deut. 6: 4–6 with the message: 'You must love God with all your heart. . . .' The inclusion of this passage shows where the emphasis is to be. The second reading is Eph. 5: 1–14, with its formidable list of possible sins, though again the message is 'Be imitators of Christ' who is the criterion of conduct. The gospel reading is either Matt. 22: 34–40 (Love God . . . love your neighbour) or John 13 (in part), the promulgation of the 'new commandment' of loving each other.[1] Thus the gospel is shown to 'complete' the teaching of the Old Testament. The gospel passages also of course emphasise love of neighbour and thus once again suggest the social nature of sin and repentance.

The 'psalm' after the first reading is Baruch 1: 15–22, a lengthy and moving 'act of contrition': '. . . we have not listened to the voice of the Lord our God but each, following the dictates of his evil heart, we have taken to serving alien gods, and doing what is displeasing to the Lord our God'. The response is 'Hear, Lord, and have mercy: for you are a merciful God.'[2]

The second model has for its heading 'Be renewed in the spirit of your mind' and includes the well-known passage Isa. 1: 10–18; verses from Psalm 50 (which echoes the Isaiah reading) and the Beatitudes in the Matthean version (5: 1–12). This last is certainly a key-text in all the matter of penance. It is at once the rule of the Christian life and the end for which all Christians ought to strive. The verse before the gospel reading is 'Come to me you that labour. . . .' (Matt. 11: 28) and is one that should be used as often as possible in penitential services.

Of the copious collection provided as alternatives we can only point out a few that one is glad to see are included. There is the repentance of David (II Sam. 12: 1–9, 13), the long series of

[1] The omission of verses in the above and other passages is a little tiresome. It makes the use of a Bible difficult. The excisions seem unnecessary in a service where one can reasonably expect people to be ready to listen. Anyway, there is nothing to stop the celebrant reading the complete passages from the Bible.

[2] The translation in the Jerusalem Bible is rather different.

readings from Isaiah, Jeremiah, Ezekiel, Hosea and others which give the deepest and most challenging teaching of the Old Testament on sin and repentance. It is precisely this doctrine with which modern Christians need to be confronted and it is reasonable to suppose that if these texts become part of their spiritual life, their practice will be transformed. In addition there are nearly forty passages from the epistles and Apocalypse and of course all the great gospel passages one would expect, including those recounting incidents of Jesus actually forgiving sinners. These are particularly important for they show us God in Christ at work in forgiveness and reconciliation.

The Order itself sums up the purpose of the readings under three heads:

1 They are the voice of God calling people to conversion and a closer conformity to Christ.

2 They show forth the mystery of reconciliation effected by the death and resurrection of Christ and by the giving of the Holy Spirit.

3 They give the message of divine judgment on good and evil in the life of mankind and thus enlighten the conscience.

All these themes are to be found in the readings and it will be necessary for the preacher to remember this.[1]

The purpose of the *homily* is clearly set out: taking the readings as his point of departure, the preacher is to remember that they convey the voice of God calling to repentance, conversion and renewal of life (24, 52). The preacher is to remind his hearers that sin is committed against God, the community, their neighbours and themselves. He is to recall to them that God's mercy is infinite and exhort them to true, interior repentance. This is to be of such sort that they will make reparation for any harm they have caused to others. The *social aspect* of sin to be brought to their attention and the need to practise love of neighbour if their 'satisfaction' is to be adequate (25).

This may seem to be rather a lot and it will not be necessary to include every one of these considerations on every occasion. The composition of the assembly and the circumstances of time and place must be taken into account. But these directives are necessary and good. Too often the recommendation of the *Constitution on the Liturgy* and those of the Order of Mass are ignored

---

[1] The emphasis in the *Ordo* on the need to build the homily on the scripture texts is very heavy and significant. This is how *all* homilies should be constructed.

and in penitential services it is particularly important that the old-style mission sermon should not be thought to be in place. Emotionalism and dramatic language and gestures leave modern people with a sense of unreality if not of the ridiculous. Nor should the homily be heavy-handed in a moralistic direction. The readings if properly chosen will suggest to the preacher the lessons he should convey and always, either directly or indirectly, he will seek to convey the 'mystery of reconciliation effected by the death and resurrection of Christ and the giving of the Holy Spirit'.

In any case the homily is at least in part a preparation for the *examination of conscience*. The homily is to be followed by a silence to allow people time to think and to make their acts of sorrow. But also the celebrant may help the penitents by reciting short sentences or even a litanic kind of prayer 'taking into account their condition, age, etc.' (26, 53).

This paragraph suggests a pretty flexible use of 'sentences' and prayers. Without ever suggesting that anyone has committed specific sins, the celebrant can give great help to people by broadening their horizons and deepening their understanding of sin. Most of us are extremely limited in our outlook on what sin is and what sins we ourselves have committed. The 'social aspect', so heavily emphasised by the Order, is one that most of us never advert to at all. How far are we responsible for at least some of the evils of our society? Do we accept evil situations just because everyone else does and because if you lift up your voice you will get disliked? This sort of thing can be put in the quite conventional categories of 'human respect' or 'selfishness'. Or on the second count, have we lost a sense of sin as something that is opposed to the holiness of God and the dignity of human beings? And in the more private sector of morals, is there not a need to point out that reconciliation between individuals, however effected, is a central requirement of the gospel? People can get all steamed up about sexual sins while at the same time failing to realise that their lives are full of bitterness and hatred. Within families it is sometimes necessary for their members to realise that forgiveness and reconciliation are the very condition of their living as Christians. How often this element is absent! Odd as it may seem, people sometimes need to be taught how to forgive.

The shaping of such a series of questions is a matter of some delicacy and it may be, as the Order recommends for penitential services in Lent for instance, that consultation with the laity will be a condition of success.[1] Immersed as they are in ordinary life, they will usually have a much more adequate and vivid sense of the evil that is to be found in modern life than the clergy and will be able to help him to frame his considerations. It is they who for example will know that racial discrimination, whether official or unofficial, is being practised in some places of work. They and they alone will know whether various forms of dishonesty are prevalent in a particular kind of job and they will know how the young and the defenceless are being treated. It may well be that the individual or even the Christian community cannot do much about such matters. On the other hand, if the community is aware of them, there is some likelihood of something being done. As we have said above, this could be the 'penance' the community accepts for itself. Among other things, such a procedure would relate the sacrament of penance to real living.

In Appendix III of the Order (p. 164) there is a scheme for the examination of conscience. It is not intended to be read out but may be used by the penitent privately. It calls for a brief consideration.

The first thing one notes is that it is based on the Ten Commandments and in general may be described as an updated version of the kind of forms for the examination of consciences to be found in the older-fashioned prayer book. It is divided into three parts, the first consisting of questions on our obligations to God: worship public and private, dangers to faith and means of preserving it and one notes the question: 'Have I paid attention to education in the Christian faith by hearing God's word, attending catechetical instruction . . . ?' Reverence for God and holy persons, oaths, come in for mention next and of course the question of attending Mass. The second and much longer section is concerned with obligations towards others, scandal, relationships in the home, sharing what one has with the poor and the defence of the oppressed, the weak, the old, etc. Again, 'Have I fulfilled the mission to which I was called in confirmation?' and 'Have I had a concern for human society in promoting social justice, good morals, and peace?' Here the modern note is sounded but when the questionnaire goes on to ask 'Have I been just, honest and industrious at work? Have I paid a just wage?' one feels that the scheme does not take account of modern conditions. Trade Unions and monster companies are not in the picture. In a

[1]See OP 40b.

47

further question, 'Have I obeyed lawful authority and given it due reverence?', one feels that the whole matter is over-simplified. There are 'lawful authorities', sometimes recognised by concordat with the church, obedience to which has led to the most frightful evils. *How* is the conscience of those who have to live under unjust régimes which have been described as organised violence against the weak and oppressed to be guided? There are acute moral problems here which are the daily concern of thousands of people who in anguish ask themselves: 'Is it right to resist violence with violence and, if I do, do I sin? Am I responsible for the deaths and injuries that may follow?'

The last part begins more propitiously: What is the fundamental direction of my love? This echoes the modern moralists' concern about the 'fundamental option' which can have a quite crucial importance in judging the gravity of sin. The questions that follow are concerned with what for too long and unhappily has been called the 'spiritual life' and if they seem new—and indeed are to be welcomed—one reflects that they appeared in a rather different context at the end of the old 'Penny Catechism'. *Plus ça change.* . . .[1] The last section (4) dealing with sexual sins is very reserved and that is a good thing.

It will be seen that the scheme is only very partially updated and reflects the conventional 'ten commandments' moral theology of the manuals which, however stretched, has exerted a restrictive influence on moral perceptions. Nor can this scheme be said to be traditional. Thomas Aquinas constructed his moral theology around the virtues and vices and not only *said* that charity is the queen of the virtues but showed that it was in the very working out of his theology. It is significant that he has remained the source of moral theology, as distinguished from casuistry, until recent times.

Nor is this scheme really related to the New Testament or indeed the deeper insights of the Old. The twofold 'law' of the gospel is indeed quoted at the head of sections **I** and **II** but it does not 'inform' the lists that follow. Among the many other much-preconised 'crises' in the church today is that of sin: what is it? What happens when you do it? What *sort* of relationship with God is broken and when? The textbook answers to these questions are no longer satisfying the people nor, for that matter,

[1] In question 2 of this section one is alarmed to see that the 'talents' of the gospel (Matt. 25: 14–30) are interpreted as 'gifts' of personality.

the theologians and the exegetes have been throwing new light (that is in fact old) on the whole matter.[1] It must be admitted that a great deal more work needs to be done and sooner or later theologians will have to construct a credible framework of Christian morality which will guide ordinary people. No doubt it will be said that the 'ten commandments' scheme does provide such a guide. It is, however, manifestly inadequate and it is a pity to perpetuate it even if it comes on what is only an unofficial part of an official document. However, it need not be used and local conferences of bishops are urged 'to complete and adapt' it to local circumstances. This, though restrictive to all appearances, leaves enough room for bishops to draw up other schemes. If they do, it is to be hoped that they bring theologians, the parish clergy, lay-people and catechists into consultation. In spite of Chesterton, Father Brown and all that, priests do *not* know everything about sin.

In the third section the last question but one reads: 'Have I acted against my conscience . . . ?' and although it limits its scope by adding 'out of fear or hypocrisy' it suggests an opening to a new way of thinking about judgment on sin. One of the most marked developments of the morality of the Old Testament was the steadily developing interiorisation of sin. At first often no more than a ritual of uncleanness, it became with Jeremiah and Ezekiel a personal interior matter. A new 'heart of flesh' had to be transplanted into the individual sinner with which he would respond in the depths of his being to the call of God. If then even the 'just' reject the call he 'dies because of this, he dies because of the evil he himself has committed'.[2] Unfortunately this profound teaching of the prophets was largely negatived by the emphasis on the law in the last two or three centuries of Judaism: 'The emphasis on observing the law led to a situation in which obedience became the sole virtue or, as one commentator has said, the cannibal virtue. The rabbinic schools came to interpret the law in ever more detail and "to build a hedge around the law", ending up with as many as 640 precepts. All this led to *an externalisation of sin in terms of the illegal act*, a matter of calibrating

[1] See for example X. Léon-Dufour, *Dictionary of Biblical Theology*, 2nd ed. (Geoffrey Chapman, 1973), s.v. 'sin' and L. Ligier, 'The Revelation of Sin in the Mystery of Christ', *International Catholic Review*, Nov.–Dec. 1973 (6/73), pp. 327–44.
[2] Ezek. 18: 26 and the whole passage vv. 21–32. For the 'heart of flesh' see Ezek. 36: 25–27 and Jer. 4: 4; 33: 8.

particular trespasses rather than of recognising the basic corruption of the will which gave to sin its deep-lying unity and coherence.'[1] This may seem to be of no more than academic interest. Unfortunately there has been a parallel development within the church since the days of the Nominalists, who held that actions were wrong because God forbade them and not because they were wrong in themselves. Sin became an almost automatic abreaction to the law and, since law can never encapsulate the whole of life, large areas of experience were left untouched. Among other things, this system led to an atrophy of the conscience which now simply had to judge whether it was responding to a given law, whether described as divine or ecclesiastical. This is why that little question on conscience is so important, for we seem to be recapitulating the experience of the past, or rather going deeper. We are more aware of sin-situations than were our forefathers (even if we are no more successful than they in overcoming them) and there is evidence of a need to interiorise even further our experience of sin. Analysing the biblical data on sin and especially St Paul, Père Ligier has this to say: 'Sin does not consist solely in the transgression of an external prescription but in an inner aberration of the mind, of which man must become aware because it estranges him from himself. Sin is, therefore, in a sense an alienation of man.' This fruitful idea, which corresponds both to the demands of conscience and of faith, is particularly welcome today. Sin is not simply a concept that is determined from outside by the play of social traditions and the tenacity and persistence of biblical views.[2]

The idea of sin is rooted in human nature, which it protects from possible abuses of freedom. *There are modes of behaviour, experiments and acts which are defective because they contradict conscience.*[3] Man becomes conscious of sin because it alienates him from himself but the Bible is necessary to elucidate the meaning of sin and the extent of sin. But it is the view here expressed that it is for conscience to judge, not merely in the light of an external code but out of the depths of the heart, that is important and this suggests that no schemes for the examination of conscience can ever be more than more or less inadequate guide-lines. One of the great tasks that lies ahead for the church is the education of

[1] Denis O'Callaghan, 'What is Mortal Sin?' in *The Furrow*, February 1974 (Vol. XXV, 2), pp. 80–1.
[2] To paraphrase: 'Sin is not sin just because the Bible says so!'
[3] *Art. cit.*, p. 330.

conscience, a process that did indeed start with Vatican II—to the great dismay of many. This development is necessary not simply because it is vaguely 'better' but because it will meet the conscientious needs of the modern Christian who has to make decisions for himself in the face of the increasing complexity of modern life.[1]

What, then, is required is a series of 'considerations', questions or even statements that will help the penitent to deepen his understanding of his own situation so that he may become more acutely aware of his condition in the sight of God. Secondly, there is a need for guidance about social morality which goes beyond the sort of question that runs 'what have *I* done or not done?' to questions that raise the whole matter of the community whether ecclesial or civil, to which the penitent belongs: 'What does the community to which I belong do or not do that it ought to do?' In this way the teaching of the Order itself—that men are solidary in sin as they are in reparation for sin—could become a reality. If no detailed suggestions are given here about such 'guides to conscience' it is because the matter is one of considerable complexity and because it is only through widespread discussion with the laity that such a guide could be drawn up. One thing is certain: a renewal in the practice of private penance and the success of the Order depend on a renewed theology of sin and a deepening of the Christian conscience.

The next section (54) is significantly called 'The Rite of Reconciliation' and equally significantly consists of a General Confession *and* prayers that are petitions for reconciliation with God and the church. The text of the General Confession is the same as that in the Order of the Mass. Of the prayers a few points are worthy of note. The deacon (or other minister) in an invitatory prays that pardon may be granted to the guilty and medicine to those wounded (by sin)—another instance of the emphasis on the 'medicinal' aspect of 'satisfaction' rather than on the penal. He goes on to ask that those who have separated themselves from the church by sin may be restored to it, that they be restored to communion at the altar and may be remoulded

[1] Was that simple Austrian peasant, Franz Jägerstätter, who resisted conscription into the Nazi army *against* the advice of the local hierarchy right or wrong? He alone, like St Thomas More, had to make the decision and in our view nowadays he was right. In his own day the prevalent view was that he was wrong.

(apparently an echo of Phil. 4: 21) in the hope of eternal glory. Again, the social aspect comes in another petition asking that those who have been renewed in love may become witnesses of God's love for the world. The whole rite is concluded with the Lord's prayer which played so important a part in the forgiveness of sins in the early church, and a collect asking that those who confess their sins may be freed from them and may give thanks to God for their interior renewal.

The second model provided is less specific but much more biblical and the response is taken from the parable of the Pharisee and the tax-collector: 'Lord, be merciful to me, a sinner.' Some of the petitions are as follows: 'you were sent to proclaim the good news to the poor and heal the contrite of heart. . . . You came to call not the righteous but sinners (to repentance). . . . You forgave her much because she loved with a great love. . . . You refused to condemn the adulterous woman but let her go in peace. . . . You promised paradise to the repentant thief' and finally, the text that underlies the whole prayer-element of the sacrament, 'Seated at the right hand of the Father, *you are always living to make intercession for us*', which evokes the response for the last time: 'Lord, be merciful to me, a sinner.'

There would seem to be no reason why at any given service petitions from both models should not be used. In this way the message and challenge of the gospel would be heard and the ecclesial and social dimension would not be overlooked.

The confession that follows is of course private but so also is the absolution. Perhaps this is for practical reasons, namely the fear that penitents might leave the service without absolution at all. But at least an alternative might have been suggested, namely the possibility of a public absolution. There has been a general expression of repentance, a common prayer for forgiveness and reconciliation and even a general confession. A public absolution would have been in line with this and the sign nature of the sacrament. If there were a danger of people going away unabsolved, this could be pointed out and the matter left to the local clergy.

The rite concludes with the thanksgiving and the dismissal (56–59). But the text leaves open wider possibilities: 'The celebrant surrounded by the other priests who have heard confession invites the people to make a thanksgiving and exhorts them to good works whereby the grace of penance may be manifested in the life of each one of them and *in the life of* the community.' This gives scope for the appointing of tasks for the service of the community which the penitents will be invited to accept as the visible 'penance' which will carry the effect of the sacrament into everyday life.

After a hymn of thanksgiving the Order provides a long and splendid prayer which is to be recited by the celebrant. It recalls the whole redeeming work of Christ from the incarnation to the resurrection and the sending of the Holy Spirit. It asks for interior renewal and that the penitents may be made more like Christ and concludes: 'We thank you for the wonderful work of your love and *with the whole church* we praise you in voice and heart and deed, singing to you a new song. To you, Father, through Christ and in the Holy Spirit, be glory now and always.'[1] As the penitents have been reconciled to the church by the power of Christ operative in the sacrament, so now with the whole church they give thanks to God for that same reconciliation.

In addition, as is now usual, a series of blessings is provided (**58, 212–14**) and a formula of dismissal.

Pastoral Considerations

As will have been seen, this is a well-constructed service, rich in content and summing up almost all of the material in the introduction. The question remains how far it is of pastoral value. There is first the difficulty of getting people in any numbers to a non-eucharistic service and even if a reasonable number could be persuaded to come, it is more than probable that the weaker brethren, precisely the ones who would best profit from it, would not be there at all. It may be that something could be done by bringing in a special preacher and by advertising the event well beforehand. The old 'mission service' seems to be dead and perhaps something could be done by devising new 'mission' services which, however, would have to be based on the liturgy that is provided here. The perfervid and emotional exhortations of the past not only do not appeal to people nowadays, but, with their concentration on sin and hell and indeed on particular kinds of sin, they are totally inadequate to express the doctrine of the revised sacrament of penance. There is evidently a good case for bringing together the parish clergy and the religious who have been traditionally associated with this kind of work and seeing if something cannot be done to work out acceptable formulas.

[1] For whole text see translation, p. 118.

53

But like every other part of the liturgy, this cannot exist in a pastoral vacuum. If such services as this are to be a 'success' they will have to be part of a pastoral effort which will reach out to people where they are. For this the full co-operation of the laity will be necessary, not only in visiting people but also in constructing the service. It is their experience and insights which will turn these services from being pieces of clerical liturgy into the expression of the life and penitence of the community. Something of the sort has been attempted in various places in recent years, but in future the planning will have to begin with the liturgy of penance and eventually return to it. It is but one more example of how pastoral practice will have to be reshaped around the liturgy.

Another smaller but intractable difficulty is the availability of sufficient priests for the private confessions and absolutions. If the service is not to be unduly protracted, a considerable number will be needed and apart from populous centres with many churches, it is difficult to see how they are to be obtained. One unhappy solution might be to use the first part of the service down to the General Confession and the prayers and then to hear the confessions and leave out all the last part. Even to suggest this is to say that the liturgy of the Order has a grave pastoral weakness and this, in the view of the present writer, is because the Congregation for Worship and the others concerned with the matter in Rome have felt that the time has not come for a general sacramental absolution with the exception of the arrangements given in Part III. It has been said[1] that the theology of the sacrament of penance is still undergoing review by the theologians and it is not for a liturgical body, however eminent, to anticipate their findings. There is the problem of the validity of absolution of unconfessed mortal sins, though the objections to such a procedure do not seem to be insuperable.[2] There is of course the question of the *advisability* of absolution without previous individual confession but this is a practical matter, the answer to which cannot dictate theological conclusions. Much if not all the church's legislation on the matter through the centuries seems to have been dictated by a *pastoral* concern and what is needed, among other things, is a clear distinction between what is pastoral concern as expressed in law and the exigencies of revelation and

---

[1] *Notitiae*, February 1974 (90), pp. 67–8.
[2] See below, pp. 59–61.

the theology that must be based on it. Whatever the theological difficulties, it remains that this service of reconciliation is pastorally much less effective than it might have been. However, the Order *has* provided a rite of General Absolution/Reconciliation and much will depend on the decisions of conferences of bishops in this respect.

CHAPTER EIGHT

The Order for Reconciling Penitents with General Confession and Absolution (31–35)

The language of the introduction here deserves particularly careful attention. The first paragraph reads: 'Individual and integral confession with absolution remains the one (*unicus*) ordinary mode by which Christians are reconciled to God *unless* physical or moral impossibility excuses them from this kind of confession.' If then private confession is the 'ordinary' mode of reconciliation there must be other modes that are to be described as 'extraordinary'. The church, then, is stating that it is within its competence to limit the manner in which reconciliation is achieved but also to extend it when circumstances so require. It would seem to follow that what is absolutely indispensable for the constitution of the sacrament is repentance, general confession, the act of reconciliation/absolution and satisfaction.[1]

Such circumstances occur from time to time and all Catholics are familiar with the practice of a General Absolution in various kinds of danger of death. These are mentioned as going without saying but the Order extends the range of circumstances in which such an absolution can be given. These may be listed as follows:

1 When there is a large number of people and there is an insufficient number of confessors so that people could not be confessed within a reasonable time (*intra congruum tempus*) and without their fault would be deprived of *the grace of the sacrament* and would *have to go without holy communion for some time (diu)*.
2 This can happen in missionary territories 'but also in other places'.
3 There may be other gatherings of people where the same need can be shown.

In (1) then there are several factors to be taken into account: an insufficiency of confessors; the question of a reasonable time of

[1] See OP 35a.

waiting; the need and desire of penitents for 'the grace of the sacrament' and deprivation of holy communion. How all these factors are to be assessed is a matter of some delicacy but the Order would seem to rule out (**31**, last paragraph) what is the most common difficulty: the large numbers of penitents on the occasion of a great festival or a pilgrimage 'when confessors can be obtained'.

However, all turns on the first factor: the provision of confessors. Let us try to look at the matter quite practically. It is Easter time. The clergy spend long, weary hours confessing large numbers of people. There may be three hundred people in the church and the priests available, two or three at the most, are occupied in the confessionals. The pressure is considerable and inevitably the confessors have a strong inclination to speed up the administration of the sacrament to the point where it becomes anything but a celebration as required by the Order. There *may* be some countries and places where there is a ready supply of confessors but in most places there is not. On the other hand, all the penitents wish to benefit from the sacrament of penance and many will need to. *All* wish to go to holy communion on Easter Day. The details of such situations could be spelt out at much greater length but it is unnecessary. Everyone, both priests and people, know all about it. There is here, it would seem, a strong case for the General Absolution and it is these situations that need to be carefully considered by the bishops whose responsibility it is (OP **32**) to decide in what circumstances the General Absolution may be given. It is not simply a question of 'giving permission'. The bishop in consultation with his fellow-bishops is to decide (*decernere*) when such an absolution may be given. There is a need for a widespread consultation too with the parish clergy and also if possible with the laity for it is they who have personal and practical experience in the matter. It is not enough to say of clergy and laity, 'Of course they would never have it. They would not think they had been really absolved.' Who knows until they are asked?

As for the last paragraph of **31** the crucial phrase is '*Cum confessarii praesto esse possunt*' (if confessors can be made available). The answer is 'Generally speaking, no'. This is true even if England still refuses to regard itself as a missionary country as France has for the last thirty years. 'Missionary territories' now exist almost everywhere and that apparently inexhaustible supply of confessors the manuals speak of are hard if not impossible to come by. With the decreasing number of priests almost everywhere, the situation is not likely to get better. Instead, then, of allowing ourselves to be dictated to by events, it would be better to anticipate the new situation when there will be an insufficiency of priests to confess the people at least on the occasion of the great feasts.

Reconciliation by general confession and absolution (all the terms should be noted) should not be regarded as an easy option. The Order requires for *validity* true repentance of sins committed, a firm purpose of amendment, the reparation of injuries to others and the intention to confess the sins in due course (*debito tempore*) (33). In other words *all* the requirements of the sacrament of penance remain with the sole exception of auricular confession on the given occasion. Even if confession at a future date still remains an obligation, the penitent will have received the 'grace of the sacrament' even if he dies before being able to confess his sins individually.

The conditions for benefiting from this kind of reconciliation are that the penitent must confess his sins in private confession before being able to profit from another similar absolution. In any case, unless there is a moral impossibility, he must do this within the year for the precept binding on all Christians who have sinned gravely to confess at least once a year is binding on them too. There is considerable scope for the casuist here. What sort of 'moral impossibility' will suffice? What is a 'just cause' excusing such a penitent from private confession before receiving validly another general absolution? Excusing causes will no doubt be interpreted broadly or strictly in different places, as has always been the case and it is probably inevitable that this should be so. The Order is a liturgical document and casuistry is not its business.

What is, however, noteworthy is that the terms of the Order are generally not restrictive and on the subject of the 'precept' it is laconic. It does not say it is a 'divine precept', though it refers back to the document issued by the Congregation for Faith of June 1972. This states that auricular confession is of 'divine precept' though the interpretation of that term is still a matter of debate. Thus Louis Monden states that though confession of individual mortal sins is said by the Council of Trent to be *iure divino*, this expression 'had not yet acquired the meaning we assign to it today and was often used for ecclesiastical and even for civil law'.[1] This chimes with what Père Tillard had

[1] *Sin, Liberty and Law* (Geoffrey Chapman, 1966), pp. 47–8.

to say after a long analysis of the debate at the Council of Trent. The debate was in fact inconclusive and Tillard goes on to say that 'the Council of Trent in its declaration *Statuit et declarat* was merely affirming *the customary law of the church*'.[1]

The question may seem to be of not much more than academic interest. It will be said that all good Catholics want to confess their sins individually. No doubt that is largely true and if they refused to do so one would be troubled about their motives and dispositions. But this does not answer the theological question: is auricular confession of mortal sins of divine law in the strict sense or is it not? As everyone knows, the answer of the Catholic church for hundreds of years is that it is. But there are one or two problems. Until the seventh century or so private confessions were unknown and earlier than that it was the common practice always to receive holy communion whenever a Christian attended the eucharist. Were all these people free from what is now called 'mortal sin'? It seems improbable. Historians tell us that as long ago as St John Chrysostom, he and other Fathers condemned non-communicating attendance at Mass but we do not know what sort of sin if any kept people away. It is also true that there was some confession of sins which could not be described as public[2] but there was no *legal* obligation to do so until the general law of the Fourth Lateran Council. Are we to suppose that the church at that time was wrong and that the modern (i.e. substantially since 1215) practice is an authentic *theological* development which is sufficient to justify it? There seems in fact to have been little enough theological reflection on the matter until the thirteenth century when the Scholastics perforce took current practice as the basis of their theology.[3] On the other hand, there is the common teaching of the theologians and the practice of Christians for more than seven centuries though this tradition too needs to be examined. Evidently the whole matter needs further reflection but one dominant feature that should be allowed full influence is the good of the people.

[1] LMD 90, 1967, pp. 117–24. He also cites the opinion of a modern moralist, Regatillo, that confession before communion and after mortal sin is to be regarded rather as an ecclesiastical precept. See *Penance: Virtue and Sacrament*, ed. J. Fitzsimons (1969), pp. 45–6, for a summary account of the debate and *Christian Celebration: the Sacraments*, p. 223.

[2] See Poschmann, *op. cit.*, pp. 85 ff.

[3] A parallel case is that of confirmation. See *Christian Celebration: the Sacraments*, pp. 89–95. It is also necessary to recall that the medieval theologians had but an imperfect knowledge of epochs earlier than the twelfth century.

The answer to the question will largely turn on the meaning of 'mortal sin'. For some time now theologians have been urging that the matter should be re-considered and seem to be agreeing that there is a difference between mortal that is, deadly sin, 'sin that is death'[1] and grave sin or serious sin.[2] The terms are not of the highest importance. What is important is that these and other theologians distinguish between the sin that is a complete turning away from God—and that is what the Bible seems to be thinking of when it speaks of sin—and the sort of sin that is by no means a rejection of God but rather a falling short of the fundamental direction of their life which is Godward. This has been called 'the fundamental option'. People whether consciously or not have chosen God and his demands but from time to time fall away from that which is the fundamental direction of their lives. There is a failure of response to the demands of God whom they have chosen and wish with all their heart to serve and, it is argued, the relationship with God is not broken. The notion that anyone after breaking the law of God on a single occasion could be 'sent to hell' for all eternity is no longer acceptable and is indeed regarded as bizarre. What sort of God would that be? On the other hand, the new notion (if it is new) contains a fundamental psychological truth: the whole personality is rarely if ever involved in one single act and yet we find it quite conceivable that a long series of wrong acts do produce a state that can be said to be alienation from God. As long then as people are holding on to their 'fundamental option' and trying to maintain union with God, even if imperfectly, it is difficult to regard them as in the state of mortal sin as it has been conventionally understood.[3]

Pastorally speaking the matter is of the greatest importance. The quasi-automatic notion of mortal sin has weighed on people of more tender consciences and produced the almost incurable disease of 'scruples'. The system operated in a very different direction also. There were those who had 'missed Mass' or broken the Friday abstinence and who thought that because they had committed one 'mortal sin', they might as well commit others of a

[1] See I John 5: 16.
[2] See Denis O'Callaghan, 'What is Mortal Sin?' in *The Furrow*, Feb. 1974 (Vol. XXV, 2), p. 82; and L. Orsy, 'Common Sense about Sin' in *The Tablet*, 9 Feb. 1974, pp. 125–8. The former speaks of 'grave sin', the latter of 'serious sin'.
[3] One of the more disturbing features of the system was the 'liberality' with which the moralists invented mortal sins. It is this as much as anything else that, one suspects, has brought the whole system into disrepute.

very different kind. A consequence of this view was that the 'sinner' was in 'a state of mortal sin' which depressed many, decreased their spiritual energy and drove some almost to despair. The young were given the impression that 'impure thoughts' or the least 'motion of the flesh' was gravely sinful and this too made them think that they were cut off from God even if they were making genuine efforts to lead a Christian life. The list could be prolonged and it must be said that in the hands of wise and compassionate confessors the evils of the system were greatly mitigated. None the less the system itself was bad and always open to abuse. Whether or not it was used wisely, it was not in accordance with the psychological facts and is difficult to reconcile with the biblical view of sin.

The foregoing considerations may seem to have little enough to do with the liturgical form of penance but the pastoral use of it is likely to be seriously affected unless this matter of sin is cleared up. It is readily agreed that it is spiritually profitable to confess in private sins that have been traditionally called 'mortal' but it may not always be so and obligation is very different from spiritual recommendation. One has to wonder how the *obligation* to confess mortal sins after a general absolution will work out in practice and how indeed in an age that is not responding to obligations in any form people will treat it. Might we not then have the wholly undesirable situation of people thinking that they are absolved from their sins, and yet who in the sight of the church are still in them? The Order does indeed speak of a 'moral impossibility' to confess mortal sins in a subsequent confession, at least within the year (34), and this presumably means among other things the unavailablity of a confessor. Again, we find ourselves up against the same problem. But there will be other excusing causes which no doubt will be discussed by the moralists in due course.

To plead, however, for some mitigation of the rule of confessing mortal sin before confession is not to plead for the abolition of private penance. In the course of centuries this has proved to be a valuable means to help people to live the Christian life and has kept alive a concrete notion of what is sin. In an age when fornication, adultery, theft and perjury seem to be almost popular pastimes, it is necessary to dot the moral 'i's and cross the 't's. If the now traditional system has preserved this sense of sin and by a curious abreaction somewhat dimmed the enormity of real sinfulness in the sight of God this is because all systems have their weaknesses. Another on the lines suggested above would also have its weaknesses. Both penitent and confessor could deceive themselves about the moral qualities of a single sinful act but laxism was by no means unknown under the current system. The balance is difficult to maintain.

The Rite (60–66)

The language of the title of this rite should again be looked at. As one writer has observed,[1] the thought behind this rite is very different from what we have conventionally understood as a 'general absolution'. It is a manner of being reconciled with God and there is much more to it than the utterance of a formula. First of all, it is a *liturgical service* which retains all the features of classical penance with only one exception: the *private* confession of sins for this occasion.

1 There is the reading of the scriptures.
2 The homily.
3 The general confession made by all those who wish to receive absolution and according to the formulas used in the other services or at Mass.
4 There is prayer, as above in the previous service, always ending with the Lord's prayer.
5 Finally there is absolution in very solemn form (**62**).

Commentary

The fact that the reconciliation/absolution is embedded in a service of the word totally changes its complexion, and at the same time gives it a pastoral importance of the highest degree. First, there is a confrontation with the word of God which will enable the participants to realise what is the evil of sin. Secondly, the homily which will naturally move towards its end into an examination of conscience will deepen and extend that realisation. The general confession here acquires its full force: the whole

[1] Austin Flannery, OP, translation of the Order in *Doctrine and Life*, April 1974 (Vol. 24, 4), p. 206n: 'General Absolution does not mean the same thing' as that intended by the Order and he has chosen 'Communal Absolution' as the title. He also points out that the terms 'reconcile', 'reconciliation' for 'absolve', 'absolution' and 'confession' were deliberately chosen and refers to *Osservatore Romano*, 8 Feb. 1974. Penance is an encounter of man with God and the Order wishes to get away from the slot machine mentality: put in a sin and get out an absolution.

gathered community expresses its sinfulness *with a view* to reconciliation and absolution which immediately follow.

The absolution which is a remarkable piece of writing invokes the Father, Son and Holy Spirit. The Father who desires not the death but the life of the sinner, who first loved us and sent his Son to save us is asked to show his mercy to us. The Son who was delivered up on account of our sins and rose to make us righteous, gave the Holy Spirit to the apostles to remit sins; 'may he (Christ) through our ministry free you from sin and fill you with the Holy Spirit'. In the Holy Spirit, given for the remission of sins, we have access to the Father and he is asked to purify our hearts, to shed his radiance on us that we may proclaim the saving deeds of him who has called us out of darkness into light. The usual formula: 'I absolve you . . .' concludes the form of reconciliation.

The first thing that may be noted about this text is that it is *prayer* and that in it is expressed by means of a catena of scripture passages the meaning of reconciliation with God and his church. Here the truth the Order wishes to emphasise—that the sacrament of penance is above all reconciliation—is made very plain. Likewise, we note the mention of the Holy Spirit in the last two passages. He is operative, he 'fills' the penitent, purifies his heart and radiates his whole being. We note too that the celebrant extends his hands over the penitents and the meaning of the gesture is interpreted by the words. As in the early centuries of the church, the laying-on of hands is the sign of the giving of the Spirit *for* reconciliation with the church. It had a peculiar significance in the reconciliation of the lapsed, the heretic and the schismatic who were regarded as having put themselves outside the ambit of the Holy Spirit's operation. For if he is the Spirit of Christ he is also the Spirit of his body which is the church.

In the event of this public act of reconciliation taking place—as one hopes it will—the use of this formula should be regarded as imperative even if the Order says that the shorter form used in private reconciliation may be used (**62**, alternative). In fact, and where time allows, there would seem to be no reason why this formula should not be used in private reconciliation. An appropriate time to use it would be the Easter confession.

Where there is urgency a shorter form may be used (**64**), though this must include a brief reading from scripture, a reminder to the penitents to be truly contrite (**60**), the imposition of the 'penance' and the general confession. If there is danger of death the reconciliation may be reduced to the formula 'I absolve you . . .' (65).

Pastoral Considerations

No doubt fears will be expressed about the advisability or pastoral effectiveness of this form of reconciliation. It will be said that people will not be able to get the personal help they need for their own particular situations. To this it can be answered that the Order requires them to make a personal confession as soon as possible afterwards and then they will be able to get the help they need. In any case, this is to underestimate the *purpose* of general absolution which is to enable people to be released from their sins, take up their Christian life once more and ordinarily to receive Christ in holy communion who will communicate *his* help to them in their renewed effort. One of the advantages of this form of penance is that it will take people away from an egocentric attitude to their sins and help them to see them and themselves in a much wider context.

It may be said that the personal encounter of penitent and confessor is a much more effective way of confronting the former with his sins and encouraging amendment of life. This is not necessarily so. Some find individual confession a great psychological strain. This may arise not so much from feelings of shame but from the intense concentration on self which such confessions require. There are others who find reflection on self almost impossible and whose subsequent confessions are remarkably laconic. These need the help that should come from this service of reconciliation and it is reasonable to suppose that they would go away from it with a profounder awareness of sin and a greater determination to do better than they do from the confessions they now make and which they often dimly feel are inadequate. If the readings were well chosen, if the homily were rightly directed, leading penitents to an examination of conscience both wider and deeper than they could ever achieve by themselves, the resultant repentance and intention to do better would be immeasurably strengthened.

All this may seem a little speculative at this time and a period of experiment would be necessary to prove that this is the case. But without the experiment we cannot have the experience on which to judge the value of this form of reconciliation. All the more reason then for the bishops to tackle this matter in a determined manner and to encourage a controlled and sufficient experiment to make it possible to assess its results. Already there is something of a crisis about the current practice of penance and it is unlikely that it will be solved by exhortations—which have never been lacking —to 'go to confession'. The dilemma seems to be this: either to allow the present situation to continue and probably worsen, with the result that fewer and fewer people will use the sacrament, or boldly and imaginatively to encourage this 'new' kind of reconciliation from which it can be reasonably forecast that more and more people will profit.

It is hardly necessary to reiterate that such an experiment would require a considerable amount of instruction or, better, a renewed education of the people in the meaning and practice of penance. But this is what the church is for and by the terms of the *Constitution on the Liturgy* (8) this is a duty that is incumbent on the pastors of the church: 'To believers also the church must ever preach faith and penance; she must prepare them for the sacraments, teach them to observe all that Christ has commanded and invite them to all the works of charity, piety and the apostolate.' This injunction is particularly appropriate to the sacrament of penance now that the Order has extended its range of reference not only to the whole Christian life of the individual but to his vocation as the bearer of the reconciling mission of the church. There is in fact a long tradition of this preaching of repentance in the church. Religious orders were founded to preach penance and conversion of life and 'missions' were a constant feature of parish life.

The church now gives the opportunity of preaching repentance and conversion within the context of the liturgy which indeed in services of penitence becomes the chief vehicle of such pastoral activity.

As we have observed above, there is the difficulty of getting people to church for non-eucharistic services and to this we may add the ingrained habit of thinking that confession is a comparatively brief affair that can be got through in a few minutes on a Saturday evening. But there is another way. At the beginning of the Mass there is a brief penitential rite and it is well known that this can be quite flexible. There would seem to be no reason why on the occasions of penitential services this should not be extended. If the Mass were in Lent, many of the scripture texts are penitential and after the opening penitential rite, these would be read and the homily would take up the penitential theme. There is nothing to stop it moving into an examination of conscience and an absolution which could be omitted at the beginning of the Mass. If allowed, the general confession and absolution could take place at this point.

Better still and, since the pattern of services of penitence is almost identical with the eucharistic ministry of the word, why should it not be allowed that the penitential service should replace the texts of the day? The service would move forward from the proclamation of the word through the homily and directed examination of conscience to (if permitted) the general confession and absolution. The people could then proceed to take part in the supreme act of reconciliation, the eucharist, in which Christ in the fulness of his redeeming activity makes himself present. If it could be shown that Saturday evenings are still (at least in some places) convenient times for confession and if the bishops of this country were to allow Saturday evening observance to stand for the Sunday observance, it is reasonable to suppose that Saturday evenings would once more become the time of the reconciliation with God and the church represented by the local community.

It is true that among the adaptions conferences of bishops may make, this fusion of the penitential service and the Mass is not explicitly mentioned, though the faculties granted under **38** and **39** are very wide and do not exclude it. The bishops may decide *when* the general absolution may be given and the clergy (**40**) may considerably adapt the penitential service both by shortening and lengthening it as well as selecting the texts. The elements for adapting the penitential service to the Mass seem to be here.

In the new missal there is a Mass-formula 'For the Remission of Sins' (*Missae ad diversa*, 40), though it does not rank as a 'ritual Mass' and it is not at all clear that it could be adapted for use with a penitential service. Nor does the Order of Penance refer to it or suggest that it should be so used. This must be said to be an oversight of both the missal and the Order. In the interests of pastoral practice and of the restoration of the sacrament of Penance to more frequent use, a clear directive would put the whole matter right. The simplest thing would be to make the Mass-formula 'For the Remission of Sins' a ritual Mass whenever it is used in conjunction with a penitential service. At the same time, the necessary adaption could be indicated.

The Order (**31**) speaks of groups of people where the need of absolution and eventual communion is present. It is difficult to know what the Order is referring to. An obvious example is the house-group which meets for discussion and the celebration of the eucharist. If this is what the Order means, then the use of general absolution becomes a real possibility. In such intimate groups it is embarrassing for some to abstain from communion and a general absolution would meet the case. Or it may be a group of teenagers who have met precisely for prayer and discussion of penance. It would not be difficult to detail other groups. If this is what the Order has in mind (and it is a pity it is not more explicit) then permissions for general absolution would need to be given quite frequently. In effect, the bishop would have to give a general permission to be used by the local clergy according to circumstances and with all the conditions required by the Order. It is to be hoped that this is the way that will be taken.

CHAPTER NINE

Penitential Services (36–37)

Specimen texts, which are not an official part of the Order, are to be found in Appendix II, 1–42. These services do not differ in form from those for the reconciliation of several people with absolution, whether public or private, but they differ in purpose. This is stated in a general way: they are a means of calling people to conversion and renewal of life and to proclaim deliverance from sin through the death and resurrection of Christ (36). More specifically, they are seen as educative or formative in the deeper sense and this is to be linked with what we have said above on this subject. They are said to be 'useful'

a to promote a spirit of penitence in the Christian community;

b to help Christians in their preparation for the individual confessions they will make subsequently;

c they are a means by which children can gradually form their conscience about sin as it occurs in human living and deliverance from it through Christ;

d they will help catechumens in the process of their conversion. Finally, where a priest is not available they will enable people to repent of their sins and through an 'act of perfect contrition' in view of a future confession to receive God's grace.

Although, then, these services have a strong educational emphasis they are also 'celebrations', as the title of the Order indicates. They are celebrations of the word of God and of its message of repentance and reconciliation which we saw above[1] is an integral part of the total gospel message. They form then part of the task of the church to proclaim God's saving mercy to the members of the church. Thus in concrete fashion their first purpose will be fulfilled. The Order indeed suggests that 'the spirit of penitence' will be developed in the Christian community and to this two further suggestions may be made. The first is that if there is to be

[1]See Chapter One.

a renewal of the practice of the sacrament it will only come about through a broadened and deepened appreciation of the biblical teaching on sin, repentance and reconciliation. Secondly, these services need not be orientated simply to the sacrament. They can very properly be made to serve the wider purpose of showing that the church is the privileged place of God's reconciliation in the world.[1] In the context of these services the relationships with others bringing with them the obligation to share their sufferings and to make what reparation is possible for their sins will be revealed.

At the same time such services will obviously help people towards a better understanding of the sacrament of penance (b). They will broaden their horizons so that they see they have a moral obligation to respond positively to certain social and even political situations. In a word, they will be a means of educating the Christian conscience.

The observation (c) that these services will help in the gradual formation of children's consciences is interesting and to this matter we shall return.

As for the practicality of these services, no doubt where there are parishes with numerous populations it will be possible to assemble a sufficient number of people for them. But why should we always think of the church as the place of assembly? Already groups are meeting in many places for prayer and for the celebration of the eucharist and these will be the occasions for the celebration of services of penitence. Such groups offer interesting possibilities. In a smaller group people's real difficulties can be ventilated and it may very well be that lay-people will be able to help each other more effectively than it is always possible for the clergy to do.[2] On the other hand, there is an opportunity for the priest to deepen the spiritual life of the members of the group in a way that is not possible in a larger assembly. It should be noted, however, that the presence of the priest is not necessary (see above). Whatever, then, may be the practical difficulties, these services provide a useful tool that should not be neglected.

The Rite

These celebrations of penitence are to conform to the pattern that is now well known and are to be along the lines indicated

[1] See OP 5, 'Reconciliation with God and the Church'.
[2] The present writer knows of such groups, of a charismatic character, where this is already being done.

by the Instruction of 1964 for Bible Services[1] though that document allows for a sufficient flexibility. In fact, the order is almost exactly the same as for the Rite for Reconciling Several People (22–30). There is an introduction, the reading of one or several passages from scripture, divided by chants, psalms or silence and there is the homily which is to explain the texts and draw out their meaning and relevance to the assembly. After the homily and meditation on the subject matter expounded, all are to pray together (prayer that may be in litanic form) ending with the Lord's prayer which may never be omitted and in which the phrase 'Forgive us our trespasses as we forgive those who trespass against us' is to be specially attended to. This could be done in the invitatory that now usually prefaces the saying of that prayer. As we have observed above, in the early church the Lord's prayer was regarded as a normal means of obtaining forgiveness of sins. The rite concludes with a collect and a dismissal.

It is interesting to note that the Order (36) allows nonscriptural passages to be used along with the Bible readings 'if they really help the community towards a true knowledge of life'. These readings may be taken from the Fathers or other writers, including, presumably, modern ones. Carefully chosen passages from St Augustine's *Confessions* and others from the *Imitation of Christ*[2] will be appropriate. But there is no reason why only 'spiritual books' should be chosen. A passage from a contemporary writer or even an incident recorded in the newspaper will serve equally well and will have an immediacy that older books usually lack.

As to the *nature* of these services, the Order is understandably anxious that they should not be confused with the celebration of the sacrament of penance (37).

Specimen Services of Penitence (Appendix II, 1–19)

The Order in Appendix II gives specimens intended principally for liturgical commissions and Christian communities to help them in drawing up such services. It takes occasion to repeat its instructions (36) and adds one or two more. They are to be adapted in style and content to specific communities and are evidently not to be concocted as 'reach-me-down' affairs that will do for anyone.

[1] *Inter Oecumenici*, nn. 37–9.
[2] See Book I (e.g. Chapter 16, 'On tolerance of other people's defects') or Book II, 'The Royal Road of the Cross'—one of the best parts of the *Imitation*.

It will also be useful to mention here that the Order (40b) recommends that lay-people should be allowed to play their part in the construction of these services. The specimens then are simply offered as models which are to be adapted to the definite and concrete circumstances of different communities. What is also to be observed is that the Order envisages here (4) the use of these services with either the Rite for the Reconciliation of Several People with private absolution or with the Rite for Reconciliation by General Confession and Absolution. We may conclude, I think, the church does not intend this last service to be a sort of permanent dead letter.

Two services are provided for Lent, 'the principal time of penitence both for the church and the individual',[1] the first presenting penance as the restoration and strengthening of the grace of baptism. The second is more directly concerned with the paschal mystery as such. The first, however, is placed within the context of the paschal mystery. *Both* services are in their different ways preparations for the celebration of the paschal mystery in the Easter Vigil. All this is very satisfactory and fully in accord with the central teaching of the *Constitution on the Liturgy*. The *teaching* to be found there is reduced to practice.

The First Service

After the usual introduction with its collect asking that as we have been redeemed by the passion of Christ we may enter into the joy of his resurrection, there follow the readings which are preceded by a brief commentary to explain their significance. The first is I Cor. 10: 1–13: as the Israelites, even after their liberation from Egypt and the favour of God that they experienced, fell into sin, so do we when we sin after baptism. The Psalm 105 (106) recalls the saving deed of God in preserving them and making them his own people in the desert. Two gospel passages are suggested, the first from Luke 15: 4–7 (the lost sheep) and Luke 15: 11–32 (the prodigal son). The Order has evidently decided to make this latter text the classical one to teach the meaning of reconciliation.

For the homily that follows the Order suggests that it might take up one or all of the following points:
the need to complete the grace given in baptism by a life of fidelity to the gospel of Christ;

[1]CL 109.

the gravity of post-baptismal sin;[1]
the infinite mercy of God who welcomes the sinner even after repeated falls (see Luke 15); or the preacher may speak about the celebration of the paschal mystery as it involves Christian initiation and the reconciliation of penitents.

These suggestions contain the whole meaning of this service and the last is particularly interesting as it refers to the following prayer of reconciliation (it is difficult to call it anything else) which is based on the prayer of the Gelasian Sacramentary formerly used in the service of reconciliation on Maundy Thursday.[2] In this text both the incorporation of new members into the church and the restoration of penitents to it are seen as effects in the here and now of the celebration of the paschal mystery.

An examination of conscience follows which may be along the lines of the formula given in Appendix III. There is always to be a period of silence for personal reflection. The Order also suggests (12) that the examination may be related to the renewal of baptismal promises that is made at the Vigil. This could certainly throw a new light on the whole matter. The global rejection of evil could be made quite concrete by relating it to the circumstances of the world in which we live (corruption in civil life, matters of social morality like abortion and so on) and the credal part of the promises could be used to underline the vocation to live in the suffering Christ, to receive into ourselves the power of his resurrection by which he overcame sin, etc. The faith element of the promises could be used to suggest a renewal of devotion to Christ to whom we promise to remain faithful in all our daily living.

In this service what is called the penitential act consists of the address of the deacon (if one is available) which is taken from the Gelasian Sacramentary and the *Asperges* with the singing (or saying) of the verse while the celebrant sprinkles the people with holy water. This represents the use of a well known symbol which is brought into use in a very appropriate context. We may note that the Order has also seen fit to (re-) introduce the posture of

[1] The text refers, not very helpfully, to Heb. 6: 4–8, which seems to exclude post-baptismal reconciliation and consigns the sinner to hell. It is a notoriously difficult passage to interpret.

[2] See for summary and partial translation *Christian Celebration: the Sacraments*, pp. 214–15. The reference there given to the Gelasian Sacramentary is 352–9, ed. Mohlberg.

kneeling at the beginning of the service (**9**), the ancient attitude of *penitential* prayer. In services that must consist largely of words these physical gestures are to be welcomed.

The prayer that follows and which is to be seen as the (non-sacramental) reconciliation/absolution is again indebted to the Gelasian Sacramentary. It offers an opportunity for a really good translation.

The service closes with a hymn and a simple dismissal.

The Second Service

This service does not differ from the former except in theme and in one detail that has some importance. After the general confession, the rubric (**19**) recommends that 'as a sign of conversion and charity towards the neighbour, some work should be proposed to help the poor so that they may celebrate the Easter festival with joy. Or visitation of the sick may be suggested or finally some effort to put right some injustice in the community.' This short passage suggests a wide range of possibilities some of which we have indicated elsewhere.[1] What is important is that here the church is indicating that the private repentance of individuals may and should have a public expression. Such a practice would not only get people's minds off their own sins or their own worries about their spiritual condition. It would carry the whole spirit of repentance and reparation into the public life of our society. It would serve to construct a *visible* sign of the church as the place and community of reconciliation. It is finally but one more indication that the church wishes to show that liturgy has an issue into life.

A further rubric (**14a**) recommends that the celebrant shall show the people that they are solidary in both sin and penitence 'so that each may realise that he is called to conversion for the sanctification of the whole community' that is, in this context, the church. This is but to take up again the teaching given before that in penance we are reconciled to the church which we have injured by sin and that our reparation can contribute to the reparation of others.

Although the resurrection is not excluded, the main theme of the service is the saving passion and death of Christ and our participation in his sufferings. Thus the first reading is Isa. 53

---

[1] *Christian Celebration: the Sacraments*, p. 220.

(in part) or parts of Psalm 21 (22) and a third reading is I Pet. 2: 20–25 (Christ suffered for you leaving you an example . . .'). The gospel is Mark 10: 32–45 which has three themes: a passion/ resurrection prophecy, the question of precedence in the kingdom of God with its message about drinking the cup of suffering and the question of authority: Jesus came not to be served but to serve others and give his life as a ransom for many.

The themes the preacher may choose in the light of these readings are set out under **17d**: sin as an offence against the church, sin as a failing in love for Christ; or the preacher can speak of 'the mystery of the vicarious expiation of Christ in which he bore our sins and by whose wounds we were healed'.[1] The social and ecclesial aspect of sin may also be dealt with and finally the paschal mystery itself which is seen as the festival by which through conversion and penitence the Christian community renews its life and so becomes a clearer sign of salvation in the world.

It will be agreed, I think, that the doctrine of this Order is admirable. The difficulty will be putting it into practice.

The service ends with the general confession, the recitation of the Lord's prayer, a collect which recalls the passion of Christ to which we have been united by penitence and in whose resurrection we hope to share. A final rubric suggests that a devotional service, like the veneration of the cross or the Stations of the Cross, may be combined with the liturgical service. This is not only in accord with the Constitution on the Liturgy (13) but witnesses to a desire to keep alive, now within a liturgical context, certain traditional practices.[2]

The Service for Advent (20–24)

The material of this service does not seem to be on all fours with the teaching in *Calendarium Romanum*, 39–42, of 1969— which apart from purple vestments and the suppression of the *Gloria* at Mass has nothing to say about the penitential aspect

[1] Possibly not everyone will be happy about the language, 'vicarious', which is only one way of looking at redemption.

[2] It must be said, however, that the Stations of the Cross need a good deal of re-thinking which must go rather further than the addition of the resurrection. There is the question of the *three* falls which drive artists around the bend and spiritual writers to repetitiousness. And the usual texts are unacceptably emotional and individualistic.

of the season. Or rather, perhaps we should say that it did not draw out this teaching, for it emphasised that Advent is about the second coming and this has a long tradition of being associated with penitence. It is this that this service brings out.

The first address recalls the twofold purpose of Advent: preparation for Christmas and expectation of the Lord's second coming 'when the history of our salvation will be completed'. Our own death is an anticipation of this event and for this we must prepare (Luke 12:37): 'May this penitential service purify us and make us ready for the coming of the Lord which we shall celebrate in the liturgy.' The prayer that follows asks that through our waiting on the Lord we may obtain pardon of our sins.[1]

The themes of the readings can be summed up: second coming/judgment (Mal. 3: 1–7), the church as the sacrament-sign of the heavenly city from which we are excluded by sin (Rev. 21: 1–12) and repentance before the coming of Christ as preached by St John Baptist (Mat. 3: 1–12 and par. Luke 3: 3–17). A strongly eschatological note is given by the insertion of the verses 'Come, Lord Jesus' and 'The Spirit and bride say "Come . . . Come, Lord Jesus"' before the gospel.

The service concludes with a collect which asks that the people may be prepared by the works of penitence to meet Christ the author of life, the Son of God, who existed before the world began.

Other Services (25–42)

Three other specimen services are provided of a more general nature. The third is particularly noteworthy for the series of intercessions based on the beatitudes which it includes. They contain in their sweep the whole range of sin, both personal and social. Simply as texts for examination of conscience they are important indications of the possibility of a different and deeper moral theology.

Services for Children and Young People (43–61)

Two services are provided for these age-groups and even if they are only models for use and appear in the unofficial part of the Order, they are important as witnessing to a concern on the part of the authorities for Christians of these ages. No doubt

---

[1] A second prayer (21) skilfully uses the Immaculate Conception of our Lady and thus integrates the feast into the penitential service.

at the pastoral level, penance for long enough has been adapted to the capacity and needs of younger people but this has been a somewhat *ad hoc* affair and the adaptations have been more or less successful in different times and places. Thus, for instance, the forms for the examination of conscience to be found in some prayer-books intended for children were quite hair-raising in that they suggested sins to children of which they would be completely ignorant. And most of them were undesirable since they took the Ten Commandments as the basis for examination. Then, in some places children of seven were made to learn the 'long act of contrition' which was beyond their comprehension or even their ability to say. These services will not prevent stupidities of that sort but they do at least give some guidelines. It is a question of *qui legit, intellegat*.

It is in fact surprising that the Introduction has no section on the confession of children and young people. The difficulties of the matter are well known and some guidance would have been welcome. Perhaps the Congregation for Divine Worship felt that the matter was beyond its competence or that sufficient guidance had been given by the Instruction of the Congregation for Sacraments of 1973 or by the appendix to the *Catechetical Directory* though both these statements were very partial. One gets the impression that Rome is still too departmentalised. Meanwhile, we must see what can be gathered from the two services provided.

First, let it be said that the mere existence of services is a sign of new thinking and is a move in the right direction. It is agreed nowadays that children come to an understanding of sin through personal relationships and this understanding is brought to light and deepened by communal services. Through this understanding, the children come to a realisation of their relationship with God in the matter of right-doing and wrong-doing and it is at this point that penance can become an act of worship. At the level of experience, it is known that it is in this way that children need to be prepared for first confession and without such preparation their understanding of the sacrament is going to be thin in the extreme.[1]

[1] This is one reason why confession before First Communion is so undesirable. Preparation for the former has inevitably to be sketchy and individualistic. Children of seven or younger can hardly profit from communal services and there is the danger of getting them to repeat formulas by rote and even lists of 'sins'. For the present writer's views on the Instruction see *The Tablet*, 11 August 1973, p. 758.

It is to be noted that the Order (43) says that the service may be used with those who have not previously been to confession. Yet it is difficult to imagine that it would be suitable to children of seven years or less, however watered down.

The form of the service is the conventional one and calls for no special comment.

After stating that its theme is 'God seeks us', the Order emphasises that the service is to be well prepared, the children are to understand its meaning and purpose, are to be rehearsed in the texts they use and in the actions they are to perform. 'Active participation' is the key-note of the service.

The children may be gathered in a church or in some other place. A class-room or school hall would be best. The celebrant is to greet them in a kindly way, remind them of the purpose of the service and of its general pattern. A hymn or other chant may be sung.

The service of the word that follows consists of a preliminary address, one scripture reading and a (brief) homily. There follows an examination of conscience led by the celebrant and adapted to the age and condition of the children. The 'act of penitence' that follows consists of a litanic prayer, which may be led by a child or children, and ends with the saying of the Lord's prayer. There is an act of contrition and firm purpose of amendment which may be expressed by some external gesture. The children may carry a candle to an altar (or something similar), light it and pronounce a formula of sorrow or they may place a written text of the prayer and the purpose of amendment on the altar. The service closes with a collect, a thanksgiving and the dismissal.

Commentary

The specimen address emphasises the twofold relationship of the human being, to God and to others: God is our Father who loves us and asks us to love him. But we must also love one another so that all may live happily together.

But we do not always do God's will. We say 'I won't obey, I will do what I want.' We do not obey God, we do not listen to his voice and 'this is what we call sin': we wander away from God and if our action is really serious we separate ourselves from him.

This is sound doctrine and is far more evangelical than 'the breaking of commandments' system which can so easily degenerate into breaking school rules.

But what does God do? He seeks us out. This is to be illustrated by a reading from Luke 15: 1–7. The passage could have been more skilfully chosen, especially if young children are in question. The introduction about scribes and Pharisees could be omitted as irrelevant to the theme and verses 8–10 added (the lost drachma) for the sake of the girls. In any case other appropriate passages may be chosen and it is well known that the parable of the Prodigal Son which follows is much loved by children. Verse 20b can be made to yield the truth that God seeks us out when we sin.

The homily, with which might well be combined the examination of conscience, is a matter that needs considerable skill, a knowledge of children and delicate handling. It may well be that the priest is not the best person to perform the service and the Order nowhere asserts that he must. It uses the vaguer term 'celebrant'. Teachers, catechists and other laity may be better equipped and if they are available the danger of confusing services of this sort with a *sacramental* celebration would be avoided. Yet many priests will wish to use such services and it would be a great pity to exclude them because they are less skilled. They, however, will have an obligation to get to know the children and acquire a certain competence in speaking to them.

The litanic prayer that is suggested is attractive and the recommendation that the children should take it over equally so. It moves from God as Father to family, to inter-personal relationships with other children and anchors the prayer to concrete situations: home, places of play and school. The refrain is appealing: '(Father), you love us and look for us'.

Of the (specimen) 'act of contrition' it can be said that it is at least simple: 'Father, I am sorry for what I have done wrong and for not doing the good I should do. From my heart I intend to do better especially . . . (in some particular way) that I may live as a child of light.' The voicing of an intention to do better in some specific way is good and necessary and children do respond to the suggestion. Moral exhortations to children usually suffer from vagueness. But the last phrase is questionable: it may well not be understood. It could easily be re-phrased 'that I may live as your child'. What is surprising is that God's love, either his for us or ours for him, is not mentioned. It is, however, only a specimen and it will be necessary to work out new forms suitable to children of different ages and places.

Much more work will have to be done not only on services of

penitence for children but on the whole question of when and how they are to go to confession. Here, as in other matters, it will be the combined efforts of the clergy, teachers, catechists and parents who will produce the most acceptable results.

The Service for Young People (54–61)

The only indication of age-grouping is given in the former service: it is intended for children of 'a younger age' (*minoris aetatis*), we may presume below twelve. This one, we may take it, is intended for teenagers.

If the question of penance for younger children has its own peculiar difficulties, this age-group has its own particular needs. At this time there is a growing understanding of sin and yet with the onset of adolescence a greater difficulty in mastering the instincts. It is an age of eruption and rebellion, an age of questioning and rejection of traditional teaching and values. Yet, it is also an age of frankness and general enthusiasm. The young of this age are willing to undertake arduous tasks and even difficult penances though they may well need wise guidance if they are so inclined. And in spite of everything, it is often an age of real prayer or the discovery of the capacity for prayer that goes beyond the recitation of formulas which is all they have hitherto attempted or even known. All these factors both negative and positive make the presentation and practice of penance easier in principle than it is for younger children. However, a great deal of insight and sympathy is necessary if people of this age are to be really helped by the sacrament of penance. Attitudes of condemnation, manifestations of shock—for the young *like* shocking their elders—will prevent an adult, whether lay-person or priest, from leading them to a more mature practice.

Since the form of the service is practically the same as the previous one we will simply consider a few of the texts.

The service strikes an optimistic note in the suggested opening address. Penitence is not simply a laborious and mournful affair. It looks to the future rather than the past (an important consideration for this age-group) and opens up for us a new way of life, leading us to the full liberty of the children of God. (That too will appeal and if the right notions are put before them, they will realise that freedom comes from the mastery of sin and the full possession of their personalities.) Christ calls us to conversion of life, offers us entry into the kingdom of his Father and puts before us the parable of the merchant who sold all he had to buy the pearl of great price. This in fact is the gospel passage suggested for the service (Matt. 13: 44–46).

The opening collect shows God as the God of light, truth and life, all notions that appeal to the young and one of the by-products of this service will be to give the young perhaps a better notion of God. He is no longer the celestial policeman on the look-out for our slips and falls and anxious to thrust us into the pit of hell. He is the God who wishes us to have life, a more abundant life and the prayer ends with the petition that by the power of the Holy Spirit we may be led to the fulness of the Christian life.

The first reading suggested is Rom. 7: 18–25, the interior struggle within us between good and evil. It is a potentially dramatic statement which represents what often goes on in the experience of the young. The mere fact that this is brought to the surface by a passage from holy scripture should bring some release. Preachers and spiritual guides have sometimes given the impression that 'perfection', especially in sexual matters, can be achieved at once. The young know they have to struggle for some degree of equilibrium and they are not helped by being told that all their wrong-doings in this respect are mortal sins.

An alternative reading is Rom. 8: 18–23 which is one of the great optimistic passages of the New Testament. The world, the whole of mankind, is struggling for perfection and the dénouement is certain though we must wait patiently, the most difficult virtue for the young. But if the homilist can take a leaf or two out of Teilhard de Chardin or the *Constitution on the Church in the Modern World*, he will be able to reveal the fundamental harmony between the natural creation and the saving plan of God. The whole of life and all the activities of youth, their work, recreation, sport, their exploration of reality are part of the *Christian* life, with the consequence that *living*, provided it is not deviant from God, can contribute to salvation.

The homilist in services such as these obviously has a very difficult task. He must know his group and he must have a sound grasp of the central things of the Christian faith. Mere moralism will just 'turn them off'. If the group is small enough it will be possible to engage in a dialogue which can be very fruitful. The young are much less inhibited than their elders and if the right atmosphere is created, they are usually willing to unburden themselves, ask all sorts of questions and examine themselves and in fact each other. If this is the situation, the priest—if he is a priest—must conduct the discussion with a light hand and throw light where it is really needed. It must also be said that where this atmosphere is created, the young wish to confess and be absolved almost at once. Confessors should be available though it is better if the priest who has conducted the service can hear the confessions.[1]

The prayer, to be led by the young people themselves and which could of course be considerably extended, stresses the main theme of the service which is renewal of life:

> Give us the grace of sincere conversion;
> Arouse in us a spirit of repentance and strengthen our resolves;
> Forgive us our sins and pardon (*indulge!*) our weaknesses;
> Fill our hearts with trust and generosity (*magnanimitatis*);
> Make us followers of your Son and living members of your church.

The text does not mention the device of allotting 'penances' though it must be assumed that this may be done. It certainly should be done for it is at this age that young people are willing to offer service to others.

A Penitential Service for the Sick

It is intended to be a communal service taking place either in church or a hospital ward or something similar. It makes no reference to either the Anointing of the Sick or to the Communion of the Sick, which is surprising. It could be a preparation for either. Nor is it easy to see in what circumstances the service should be used. Hospitals in this country are not run by religious bodies and religious services of this kind are out of the question. Perhaps old people's homes run by Catholics would provide a suitable locale. The Order (**62**) shows itself to be aware of the condition of the sick and the service must be adapted to them.

The theme of the service is 'A Time of Illness is a Time of Grace' though this is specified in the course of the service to mean the 'compassion' of the sick with the sufferings of Christ. Two features of the service call for comment.

[1] As we have suggested above, the General Confession and Absolution may well be appropriate for such a group.

81

1 The questions to assist in an examination of conscience cover very adequately the needs and difficulties of the sick:

In times of difficulty, depression, etc., do I trust in God's goodness and providence?

Am I sorry for myself and give way to feelings of despair?

Do I use my time to review my life and to pray?

Do I see my illness and sufferings as a means for suffering with Christ who redeemed us by his passion?

Do I see that my sufferings can contribute to the good of the church?

Have I a care for others who suffer along with me? Do I think of *their* needs?

Am I grateful to those who look after me?

Do I give a good example?

Am I sorry for my past sins and do I accept my sufferings in expiation of them?

These questions, apart from their inherent value, will supply useful considerations for the homily. Similar lists of questions in other services would have been useful but it remains for local communities to work them out.

2 The second feature worthy of note is the prayers suggested after the general confession. These take up and extend the notions of the examination of conscience and turn them into prayer. They are really an 'act of contrition' in which the saving work of Christ is in the centre of the picture. Again, this formula is so good that it might be used in other services as well. In fact, the impression left by the texts is that they are the work of someone who has a deep understanding of sickness and pain. This impression is reinforced by the form of thanksgiving: God of comfort and Father of mercy, you forgive the sins of those who confess to you; We praise and bless you. And so on three times.

Whatever may be the practicalities of the case, this service suggests valuable notions for use with single sick people and clergy and laity will want to use them once they are known.

CHAPTER TEN

Adaptation 38-40 and some Practical Points

Like almost all the new rites provided by the church in recent years, the Order of Penance will need a considerable amount of adaptation if it is to be pastorally effective. In no area of liturgical practice are people's habits so fixed as in the practice of penance and they will be all the more difficult to change. The Order presents a vision of the sacrament that is both wider and deeper than people have been accustomed to for many centuries. So, first, a vast amount of teaching will have to be done in all possible teaching situations and the most important of these is the school where children have learnt certain attitudes to penance which have stuck to them for the rest of their lives. If the impression continues to be given that penance is an entirely individualistic affair and that there is narrowly limited categorisation of 'sins' which can be ticked off, the new Order will not be able to work. If what the Order itself calls the 'social dimension' of sin and reparation is not taught, again it will be ineffective. And this is why there will have to be services of penance, for it is difficult to conceive that people will realise the implications of sin and of their membership of the body of Christ unless and until this is expressed in a communal liturgy. There is all our experience with the liturgy of the eucharist to show that this is true.

But if this is to be brought about, a great deal of thinking is necessary that will go a good deal beyond the translation of the texts. The Order emphasises again and again that the liturgy of penance is to be adapted to the circumstances, psychology and age of those for whom it is intended. It is indeed laid on conferences of bishops as a duty to adapt the whole Order to the needs and conditions of their region (38). The 'regulation of the administration of the sacrament of penance' which is spoken of in the same place goes far beyond matters of jurisdiction, reservations of sins, etc., which are already normal practice and which are also mentioned. The bishops will have to encourage both laity and clergy as strongly as possible to arrange and celebrate services of penance and give their liturgical commissions the opportunity of working out suitable services. Those in the Order are only models, and while the pattern suggested is obviously the right one, the details and especially the language will need to be adapted to local circumstances. Even for the practice of private penance it will be necessary to provide an adequate booklet that contains as much of the material of the Order in this respect as possible. The parish clergy should make these readily available whenever confessions are heard in church. Penitents will need to have them in their hands even in the confessional (another reason for adapting the latter) if the rite as given in the Order is to be carried out.[1]

As for when communal services of penance are to be celebrated, we have said sufficient about this above, though on further reflection the notion of services of penance combined with sacramental absolution and the Mass makes all the stronger an appeal. If we want to be really practical it is this sort of service that will bring people to church.

Among the matters that are within the competence of conferences of bishops to decide is the place of confession. The existing Code of Canon Law (908–10) lays down that the confessional must be in a conspicuous place and that there must be a grille between the confessor and the penitent. Men's confessions may, however, be heard anywhere; women's (normally) only in the confessional. This is as things are but the commentators are already beginning to talk of other arrangements. Thus, it is pointed out that the Order prescribes nothing on the subject of the place of penance or on the posture of the confessor: 'directives about these matters can be given more suitably by conferences of bishops'.[2] The same writer also observes that the laying-on of hands is a *visible* sign and should be seen by the penitent whom it concerns. He also suggests that the penitent should be kneeling or bowed and the confessor standing: 'all of which is difficult to combine with the existence of the grille'. As long as confessionals remain dark and impersonal—though many if not most may

[1] Of course wind will be tempered to shorn lambs. People of failing sight, those who do not handle any sort of book with ease, can be left in peace. Here the confessor himself will recite one or two of the texts even if they are supposed to belong to the penitent.

[2] See F. Sottocornola, *loc. et art. cit.*, p. 72.

prefer this—it will not be possible to make the gesture visible. But there has been much discussion in recent years about 'confession rooms' where confession can be combined with spiritual direction and where consequently the actions of the confessor would be visible. If there is a real desire for this arrangement, it will mean that there will have to be some architectural changes in our churches. But why not go back to the medieval custom of confessing people either in the chancel or a side-chapel? There the penitent could kneel and need not necessarily face the confessor who for the absolution could stand and hold his hands over the penitent while pronouncing the absolution. Provided the church is not too small, there would be no danger of the confession being overheard and the rite would at the same time be visible not only to the penitent but to others who are in church. If penitents wished for the conventional 'box' this would have to be available. Obviously a certain amount of thought needs to be given to the matter but the conclusions should not be anticipated: 'People do not want it.' How do we know, unless we make some enquiries and allow some experiment?

Likewise, the bishops are to suggest appropriate gestures on the part of the penitents for the service of public reconciliation/absolution. The Order (35) states that the celebrant is to invite those who wish to receive the general absolution to indicate that they do so by a sign: either by bowing the head or by kneeling down. There is no problem about this on the assumption that the assembly is already standing. Since this part follows on the homily (60), the people will be sitting and it will be for the celebrant to ask them to rise and suggest to those who wish to receive absolution to kneel down. This is likely to be the whole assembly and if so, all the better. But it is difficult to think of other suitable gestures unless there are countries and cultures where breast-beating is still a credible sign of repentance.

The next matter that is within the competence of the bishops' conferences is of very great pastoral importance. It is their duty to prepare texts 'truly adapted to the language and character of their people and apart from the "form" to compose new texts either for the people or the ministers' (38c). This gives the bishops enormous scope but it also lays upon them a considerable burden. It is to be hoped that they will invite and secure the collaboration of pastoral priests, teachers and lay-people and it is to be expected that a series of texts will be issued gradually since it is improbable that satisfactory ones will be devised the first time round. It must be said that the pastoral success of this new Order will largely depend on what is done in this matter. The church has put in our hands an instrument of high pastoral quality. Its prayers, or others based on them, distributed in popular booklets could gradually transform the all too superficial and narrow views that most people have about the sacrament of penance.

At the same time, it is to be hoped that in the process of adaptation there will be no watering down of quality. The prayers and other texts of this Order in Latin are splendid pieces of liturgical writing. The message is rich and the difficulty is not their content but that of translating them into an English that is going to speak to people of today. It is the thought and doctrine of the texts that needs to be seized upon and then expressed in our own idiom.

A small but important example is the 'act of contrition' (45) to which we have already referred. It is jejune, it does not mention the 'social dimension' of sin so much emphasised elsewhere by the Order and it gives an impoverished notion of God. A phrase like 'the highest good' may mean something to philosophers but little enough to the ordinary Christian. Finally, apart from the concluding phrase, there is no mention of Christ by whom in fact we are redeemed and through whom alone we can be reconciled with the Father. I do not think there is any case for putting this prayer into circulation. There are the alternatives (85–92) which are profoundly Christian in the sense that they so often reflect or even use the gospel. It is these that should be propagated, for prayers are among other things teaching devices (*lex orandi lex credendi*) and if people are to have a richer and deeper appreciation of repentance, it will be largely given by the right kind of prayers.

Perhaps the most important obligation of conferences of bishops and individual bishops in their own dioceses is the regulation of the use of the general confession and absolution. It is they who are to decide within the limits of the documents of the church when this rite may be used.[1] This permission, it seems to the present writer, should not be interpreted narrowly or negatively rather along the lines that 'in our country the need does not and will not arise'. The Order evidently intends it to be used. It is not just a formality in a book. What is required is a period of listening and investigation. It is not sufficient just to

[1] The footnote refers not to another part of the Order but to the Pastoral Norms of the Congregation for Doctrine, July 1972.

ask a number of like-minded and possibly uninformed people, whether clerical or lay, whether 'the people' want or need communal absolutions. There is need for a genuine discussion, based on the teaching and purpose of the Order, out of which should emerge the real desires and needs of the people. Such a discussion would at the same time be a process of education which nowadays is always necessary if liturgical rites are to be used as intended.

The powers of the parish clergy are of course limited both by the decision of the conferences of bishops and by the directives of their own bishop but it is clear (**40a**) that they are required to make the ministry of penance, according to the new Order, a reality in their parishes.

'The celebration of penance is to be both rich and fruitful' (*ibid.*)—that is the purpose of their labours and it is for them to adapt the texts both to individuals (and that does not mean suppressing what may be inconvenient to the confessor) and to the communities that take part in services of penance.

Another principle, mentioned in the same paragraph (**40b**), that is when arranging services of penitence in the course of the year he should consult the laity, is applicable throughout. With them he may choose texts, whether for readings or for prayers, that will be truly appropriate to the assembly that is to take part. The Order goes on to say that this is particularly important for children, the sick and other special groups. The prayers and other texts will have to be re-thought and what is produced should be acceptable to the people for whom they are intended. In the matter of penance we have to do with people in the most ordinary circumstances of their life. They will not be looking for high-flown English, much less for ecclesiastical-technical English. They will be looking for a language that speaks to their condition and helps them to repent and come closer to God.[1]

---

[1] There is indeed a problem here. The jargon of penance with its 'acts of contrition' and all the unreal language they are cast in may be said to be popular. In the sense that people know no other that is true. But in this Order there are a number of terms for which we have to find genuine equivalents. Thus throughout this book I have found it frequently necessary to use 'repentance' for 'contrition' and the term, a key one of the whole Order, 'reconciliation' can hardly be said to belong to the 'Catholic' vocabulary. The Order in fact makes clear that 'penance' is a process that begins in the proclamation of God's word, goes on to repentance and what I have called 'amendment of life' of which the sign is 'satisfaction' (of dubious English quality) itself usually called 'the penance'! There is much to be done here in the way of creating a new language.

Finally (40c), the clergy may, in a case of urgent necessity, decide to give general absolution to several people at once. He must later inform his bishop of the circumstances and of the fact that he has given such an absolution. Nothing surprising in that, but the local clergy will be encouraged to give such an absolution or inhibited from doing so by the general attitude and policy of the conferences of bishops.

It is not easy to say at this time what constitutes 'urgent and serious' necessity. We can take it for granted that flood or fire will justify the general absolution but as we have seen the Order does not restrict its use to these circumstances. The urgency will arise from pastoral situations and the degree of urgency will have to be assessed by the parish priest or the local clergy. The *principle* would seem to be: are there people who *need* absolution and will be deprived of it unless they can receive it together? An even greater urgency would be if people were to be deprived of holy communion, either for some time or for a long time. With the increasing scarcity of priests, there is no longer a remote possibility. To put the matter in another way, *salus populi suprema lex* (the highest law is the salvation of the people).

The times for the celebration of the sacrament of penance are obviously under the control of the parish clergy and the Order urges that these times should be made known—which is usually done—and it repeats the injunction that normally confessions should not be heard during Mass. Lent is a special time of penitence when services should be held and people given the opportunity of being reconciled with God and their neighbour (13). The Order offers a hint that at the beginning of Lent the clergy should *call* people to repentance. This is something that might be done more effectively than it is at the moment and should not be limited to telling people to make their 'Easter Duties'. Other means of making the message heard need to be used, for it is not the people in church who for the most part need to hear it. Once again, the liturgy suggests pastoral action.

The liturgical vestments used in this country (14) are usually the cassock and the stole. If the sanctuary or a chapel were found acceptable places for penance, it would be better for the priest to wear alb (or surplice) and stole. However unusual the notion, he is *celebrating* a sacrament.

Final Reflections

No doubt it will be said that this new Order of Penance is unwelcome and unpractical, unwelcome because both confessors and people have firmly fixed habits in the matter of confession, and unpractical because all that business of greeting and reciting formulas and reading scripture texts will take far too much time. As for the first, the question is not whether the habits are fixed or not but whether they are good or bad. If the latter, they ought to be changed and this Order offers us the opportunity to change them. If it had been said in 1960 that the Mass would be in English by 1970, that the people would be praying and making responses aloud, no one would have believed it. Habits and attitudes can be changed and from time to time need to be. Like all the new Orders, this is based on sound doctrine and presents a fuller and richer teaching than most people have known in our time. But if that doctrine is to become theirs, it must be reduced to practice and that can only be done by a better celebration of penance. It needs to be realised that we are celebrating the paschal mystery and not just shovelling out or collecting absolutions. The sixty-second 'confession' is just as much an abuse as the fifteen-minute Mass so much loved by some people of long ago.

This brings us to the second point. It can be granted that a period of adjustment to the new Order will be necessary and, as we have said often enough throughout this book, adequate texts for both confessors and people will be necessary if they are to *celebrate* the sacrament. But is it too much to ask that penance, which is the sacrament of the reconciliation of Christ, should be celebrated in a manner worthy of it? Is it too much to ask that a sacrament whose validity depends on the repentance of the sinner should be celebrated in such a manner that the confessor uses the means provided by the church to secure that repentance? After a period of adjustment, I imagine that both confessors and people will realise that the celebration of the sacrament is much more fruitful if even the simple formula of the individual cele-bration is used *in full*.

It may be said, it *will* be said, that the extra time it will take makes the administration of the sacrament in certain circum-stances intolerably long. Each parish will have to work out its own salvation in this respect and some alteration in the timetable may well have to be made. But where there is in fact a very large number of people requiring the sacrament, it will be for the parish clergy to make known their needs to the bishops. Unless my reading of the Order is wildly wrong, the church intends that the public reconciliation of penitents by general confession and absolution should be *used* and if pastoral circumstances show that even the private administration of penance in its new form is imposing strains on confessors and inconvenience on the people, the pastoral clergy should press for the use of that rite. In any case, hurried and sketchy administrations of penance are against the spirit of the Order.

The Order also suggests in more than one place that the confessor should give spiritual counsel or direction. This has always been the recommendation of the pastoral manuals of the past. It provides certain difficulties. Some all too evidently do not wish for it, others are so laconic that it is difficult to say any-thing to the point, but there has been a growing desire for it in more recent years and confessors should do what they can to meet the need. The observation of the Order (**10a**) on the 'dis-cernment of spirits' and the need for the confessor himself to pray for guidance has a high importance. But at the same time, such spiritual counsel in the crowded circumstances of, say, a Saturday night before a great festival is hardly possible. It will be necessary to indicate in one way or another that times will be provided for a more leisurely administration of the sacrament when people can receive the help and guidance they need.

It is altogether another question whether spiritual counsel should always be combined with confession. In parish life this is often necessary if it is to be given at all. On the other hand, there are occasions when the procedure is curiously reversed. People come to the presbytery for advice or to sort out their problems and during the course of a long conversation they 'make their con-fession', perhaps unwittingly. Such an interview usually proves to be both valuable and helpful and the subsequent act of con-fession, if they wish to make a confession, is all the easier. The counsel that can be given in such circumstances is almost always far more helpful than that given in the confessional which too often acts as a barrier to a free exchange of views.

All this would seem to point to the fact that we need to be a great deal more flexible in our pastoral methods if the sacrament of penance and the counsel that should go with it are to be as helpful to people as they should be. Perhaps we should be more willing to give time to listening to people and less to the innumerable activities that are expected of us by the people or by superiors. Some priests heroically practise the policy of the open door and a very good thing too. But you have to be pretty tough to stand the strain it imposes.

To return to the rites provided by the Order, it must be said that the second, which envisages a public service of penance with private confession and absolution, has in certain places been tried and found wanting. Liturgically and theologically there is the curious conflict between the public and the private aspects of the celebration and all the practical difficulty of getting a sufficient number of priests to hear the individual confessions. It is improbable that this new Order will do much to solve these problems.

It must be said too that there has been widespread disappointment over the unwillingness of the Roman authorities to make the public service of reconciliation with general confession and absolution a reasonably practical way of celebrating the sacrament. It has indeed opened the door to its use but the stipulation of subsequent private confession 'in due course' or at least within the year, rather negatives its practicability. One cannot but wonder whether people (for instance, the 'Easter duty' category) will confess their sins privately or will even remember to do so. Yet the Order makes this a condition of *validity* for the use of the General Absolution. It is conceivable that this will inhibit conferences of bishops in giving their permissions and then we shall be back where we were before. If that is not the case, then there will be a spate of a new and undesirable casuistry.

The reason for the Roman reserve may well be, as we have noted, the somewhat indeterminate condition of theological reflection on penance. In that case, we must remain hopeful but *at the same time* we must be allowed to use the General Absolution (according to the terms of the Order) and gather pastoral experience while doing so. A policy of 'do nothing' will not help the cause of theological development and will certainly not benefit the people for whom this sacrament as all others exists.

Decree

Our Lord Jesus Christ brought about reconciliation between God and men through the mystery of his death and resurrection (see Rom. 5: 10). This ministry of reconciliation was committed by the Lord to his apostles and his church (II Cor. 5: 18 ff), which performs that ministry by proclaiming the good news of salvation and by baptising men with water and the Holy Spirit (see Matt. 28: 19).

Through human frailty, however, it happens that Christians abandon the love they had at first (see Rev. 2: 4) and the friendship that united them to God is broken through sin. Therefore the Lord instituted a special sacrament of penance for the forgiveness of sins committed after Baptism (see John 20: 21–23), which the church has used throughout the centuries, in varying forms, but which in its essential elements is always the same.

The second Vatican Council laid down that the rites and formulas of penance should be examined, so as to bring out more clearly the nature and the effect of the sacrament.[1] The Sacred Congregation for Divine Worship has therefore prepared a new *Ordo Paenitentiae*, so that the sacrament may be better understood by the faithful.

To bring out the communal aspect of this sacrament, the new Order contains not only a service for the reconciliation of individual penitents, but also a service for that of a group of penitents, which allows for individual confession and absolution in the framework of a celebration of the word of God. A service for the reconciliation of a group of penitents with general confession and absolution has also been drawn up, for use in special cases mentioned in the pastoral rules for general sacramental absolution,

[1] Vatican Council II, Const. *Sacrosanctum Concilium*, n. 72: AAS 56 (1964), p.18.

given by the Sacred Congregation for Doctrine of the Faith on 16 June 1972.[1]

The church strives for a continual conversion and renewal on the part of the faithful. She wishes that those who have lapsed after baptism should acknowledge the sins they have committed against God and against their fellow men. She wants them to be truly penitent in their hearts, and she exhorts them to attend these penitential services as a preparation for celebrating the sacrament of penance. Therefore, this Sacred Congregation has drawn up the rules to be observed in these services, and offers some specimen services which the episcopal conferences may adapt to their local needs.

His Holiness Pope Paul VI has approved the *Ordo Paenitentiae* prepared by the Sacred Congregation for Divine Worship, and ordered its publication, so that it may take the place of the penitential rites hitherto in use in the Roman Ritual. When this Latin text has been translated into the vernacular, and the translation has been approved by the episcopal conference and confirmation has been obtained from the Holy See, the episcopal conference will then decide on the date that the *Ordo Paenitentiae* is to be put into use.

Given by the Sacred Congregation for Divine Worship, 2 December 1973, the first Sunday of Advent.

By special mandate of the Supreme Pontiff

Cardinal Villot,
Secretary of State

✠ A. Bugnini
Archbishop tit. Diocletianen
Secretary of the Congregation

[1]See AAS 64 (1972), pp. 510–14.

Penitential Services

I Introduction

The mystery of reconciliation in the history of salvation.

1 The Father has showed his mercy by reconciling the world to himself in Christ, making peace through the blood of his cross, both as to the things that are on earth and the things that are in heaven.[1] When the Son of God became man, he lived among men so as to free them from the slavery of sin[2] and call them out of darkness into his marvellous light.[3] For this reason he began his work on earth by preaching penitence with the words: 'Repent, and believe the good news' (Mark 1: 15).

This call to repentance, heard in the words of the prophets, was repeated in the preaching of John the Baptist, who came 'proclaiming a baptism of repentance for the forgiveness of sin' (Mark 1: 4). Thus were the hearts of men prepared for the coming of God's kingdom.

Jesus, however, not only exhorted men to repent so as to leave their sinful ways and turn to God with all their hearts.[4] He himself welcomed sinners and reconciled them to God.[5] Moreover, he healed the sick, as a sign that he was able to forgive sin,[6] and finally died for our sins and rose again for our justification.[7] On the night that he was betrayed, at the beginning of his redeeming Passion,[8] he instituted the sacrifice of the new covenant in his blood for the remission of sins,[9] and after his Resurrection he sent his Holy Spirit on the apostles, giving them the power of binding and loosing men's sins.[10] Theirs was to be the task of preaching repentance and forgiveness of sins to all nations.[11]

The Lord said to Peter: 'I will give you the keys of the kingdom of heaven: whatever you bind on earth shall be considered bound in heaven; whatever you loose on earth shall be considered loosed in heaven' (Matt 16: 19). Obeying this injunction, Peter preached: 'You must repent, and every one of you must be baptised in the name of Jesus Christ for the forgiveness of your sins' (Acts 2: 38).[12] From that time the church has never ceased to

94

call men to turn from sin, and to manifest Christ's victory over sin by the celebration of penitential rites.

2   This victory over sin is evident primarily in baptism, whereby our unregenerate nature is crucified with Christ, so that the sinful body may be destroyed and we may no longer be the slaves of sin but, rising with Christ, live our lives for God.[13] For this reason the church proclaims its faith in: 'One baptism for the remission of sins.'

In the sacrifice of the mass, Christ's passion is re-enacted, and the body that was given up for us, and the blood that was poured out for the forgiveness of our sins, are offered again by the church for the salvation of the whole world. In the Eucharist Christ is present, and he is offered as the 'victim whose death has reconciled us to yourself[14] so that we may be brought together in unity by the Holy Spirit'.[15]

But furthermore, our Saviour Jesus Christ instituted the sacrament of penance in the church, when he gave to his apostles and to their successors the power to forgive sins, so that the faithful who fall into sin after baptism may be renewed in grace and reconciled.[16] As St Ambrose says, the church has water and tears, 'the water of baptism and the tears of repentance'.[17]

II   The Reconciliation of Penitents in the life of the Church

3   The Church is holy, and yet always in need of purification

'Christ loved the church and sacrificed himself for her, to make her holy'(Eph. 5: 25–26), uniting her to himself as his bride.[18] She who is the fulness of his body, has been filled by him with divine gifts[19] and through her, truth and grace have been poured out to all men.

But the members of the church are subject to temptation, and often unhappily fall into sin. Wherefore, while Christ 'holy, innocent, undefiled' (Heb. 7: 26) knew nothing of sin (II Cor. 5: 21), but came to expiate only the sins of the people (see Heb. 2: 17), the church, embracing sinners in her bosom, is at the same time holy and always in need of being purified, and incessantly pursues the path of penance and renewal.[20]

4   Repentance in the life and liturgy of the Church

The people of God continue this work of repentance in many

95

different ways. They share the sufferings of Christ through patient endurance,[21] they do works of mercy and charity,[22] striving always more and more to live according to Christ's gospel, and so they become a sign to their fellow men of all that conversion to God implies. This is what the church expresses and celebrates in her liturgy when the faithful confess themselves to be sinners, and pray God's forgiveness for themselves and for others. This takes place in penitential services, in the proclamation of God's word, in prayer, and in the penitential rite of the mass.[23]

In the sacrament of penance, the faithful 'receive from God's mercy the forgiveness of their offences against him. At the same time they are reconciled with the church, which they have wounded through their sins, and which strives for their conversion through charity, example and prayer.'[24]

5   Reconciliation with God and the Church

Because sin is an offence against God which disrupts our friendship with him, penance 'is designed to make us love God and to entrust ourselves to him'.[25] A sinner who through God's grace and mercy sets out on the way of penance is returning to the Father 'who first loved us' (I John 4: 19), to Christ who gave himself up for us,[26] and to the Holy Spirit who has been generously poured out in our hearts.[27]

But 'through a wonderful dispensation of God's goodness, men are joined together by a supernatural necessity, by which the sin of one is harmful to others, just as the holiness of one individual is of benefit to others'.[28] In this way, penance always implies reconciliation with one's fellow men, who have suffered the effects of one's sin.

Furthermore, men often co-operate in wrong-doing. In the same way, when they do penance they help each other. Being delivered from their sins by the grace of Christ, they work together with all men of good will to achieve justice and peace in the world.

6   The sacrament of penance, and the various parts of which it consists

When a disciple of Christ, being moved by the Holy Spirit, goes to confession after he has sinned, he must turn to God with his whole heart. This inward change of heart, which involves contrition for his sin and a firm purpose of amendment, is expressed by confession to the church, due satisfaction and the actual amendment of life. God imparts his forgiveness by means of the church, and this is carried out by the ministry of the priest.[29]

6a Contrition
It is of the first importance that the penitent should have contrition, which is 'the sorrow from the heart for sin, and detestation of the sin committed, together with the resolve to avoid sin in the future'.[30] We must make our way towards Christ's kingdom through 'metanoia', which means a change of heart and way of life. The love and holiness of God, manifested in his Son and generously imparted to us, thus become the dominant influence in a Christian's life, and in all his thoughts and judgments (see Heb. 1 : 2; Col. 1 : 19 and throughout; Eph. 1 : 23 and throughout).[31] The reality of repentance depends on this heartfelt contrition. Conversion must affect a man inwardly if he is to be progressively enlightened and conformed to Christ.

b Confession
The sacrament of penance requires that there be confession, which comes as a result of the penitent's self-knowledge before God, and his contrition. Both the inward examination of conscience and outward accusation of faults must be carried out in the light of God's mercy. Confession requires that a penitent should be willing to open his heart to God's minister, who is acting in the person of Christ, and who pronounces spiritual judgment by reason of the power of binding and loosing symbolised by the keys of St Peter.[32]

c Satisfaction
True conversion is made complete by satisfaction for the faults committed, amendment of life, and reparation of any damage caused by the sin.[33] The measure of satisfaction required of the penitent must be proportionate to his sin. That order which has been harmed must be restored and the sickness responsible for the sin must be healed by means of a suitable remedy. The punishment of sin should be seen as a remedy, and a certain renewal must take place in the life of the penitent. Thus the penitent forgets the past (Phil. 3 : 13) and strains ahead for what is still to come, as he finds himself taken up once more into the mystery of salvation.

d Absolution
When the sinner manifests his repentance to the church's minister

in sacramental confession, God's forgiveness is granted him by the sign of absolution, and thus the sacrament of penance is completed. According to the plan by which 'the kindness and love of God our saviour for mankind were revealed'[34] God wishes to bring us salvation by means of visible signs, and renew the covenant that we have broken.

Through the sacrament of penance, the Father welcomes the son who returns to him. Christ places the lost sheep on his shoulders and takes it back to the flock. The Holy Spirit sanctifies his temple anew, so that he may inhabit it more fully. All this is made evident by a renewed and more fervent participation in the Eucharist, and the church rejoices in the return of each prodigal son.[35]

7 The necessity and usefulness of this sacrament

The wounds of sin are many and varied, both for the sinner and the community. Likewise, repentance offers us a number of remedies. For the one who has abandoned his loving union with God, penance calls him back to the life he has lost. For the one who falls constantly into venial sin through weakness, a frequent recourse to the sacrament of penance will bring strength, and will lead him to the fulness of freedom of the sons of God.

a If the sacrament of penance is to act as a saving remedy, the penitent must be disposed, through the mercy of God, to confess to a priest each and every grave sin that he can remember, having examined his conscience.[36]

b A frequent and diligent use of this sacrament is also very useful for overcoming venial sins. It is not a merely ritualistic repetition, nor a psychological exercise, but an assiduous effort towards the fulfilment of the grace of baptism. 'We carry with us in our body the death of Jesus, so that the life of Jesus, too, may always be seen in our body.'[37] In this type of confession, the penitent, while accusing himself of venial sins, should aim especially to be conformed to Christ, and to be obedient to the voice of the Spirit.

In order that this saving sacrament should exercise its full power in the lives of the faithful, it must take root in them and so urge them to a more fervent service of God and of their fellow men.

The celebration of this sacrament is an action in which the church proclaims her faith, gives thanks to God for the freedom wherewith Christ has made us free,[38] and offers her life as a spiritual sacrifice to the praise of God's glory as she hastens on her way to meet Christ.

III The Ministry of Reconciliation

8 The function of the community in celebrating penance
The whole church, as a priestly people, has its part to play in the work of reconciliation entrusted to it, and this it does in several ways. Not only does it call sinners to repentance by preaching the word of God, but it also intercedes for them and cares for them as a mother, so that they may acknowledge and confess their sins, and so receive mercy from God, who alone can forgive sin. Moreover, the church is the instrument by which the sinner is converted and absolved through the ministry given by Christ to his apostles and to their successors.[39]

9a The minister of the sacrament of penance
The church exercises the ministry of penance through her bishops and priests, who call the faithful to repentance by preaching the word of God to them, and declare their sins forgiven as they absolve them in the name of Christ and by the power of the Holy Spirit.

In the exercise of this ministry, priests act in communion with their bishops, sharing in their office and power. The bishop directs his priests in all matters concerning the ministry of penance.[40]

b In order to be able to administer the sacrament of penance, a priest must have the faculty to absolve according to canon law. All priests, however, even those who have not been approved to hear confessions, may validly and lawfully absolve any penitent who is in danger of death.

10a The pastoral exercise of the ministry of penance
In order to fulfil his task properly, a confessor must learn to recognise the diseases of the soul and so be able to apply the appropriate remedies. He must acquire the requisite knowledge and prudence to be able to act as a wise judge, by means of diligent study under the guidance of the church's teaching

authority, and especially through prayer. The discernment of spirits consists of a deep knowledge of the works of God in the human heart, and is a gift of the Holy Spirit and one of the fruits of charity.[41]

b A priest should always be ready to hear the confessions of the faithful whenever this is reasonably required of him.[42]

c The priest is acting as a father when he welcomes a penitent sinner and leads him to the light of truth. He reveals the heart of God the Father to men and acts in the image and likeness of Christ the good shepherd. He must remember that he has been entrusted with the work of Christ, who fulfilled his redeeming task with mercy, and whose power is present in the sacraments.[43]

d Since the confessor, as God's minister, is aware that he knows the secrets of his brother's conscience, he has a strict obligation to observe the sacramental seal of confession as something most holy.

11 The penitent
The penitent's part in this sacrament is of the greatest importance.

When, being properly disposed towards this saving remedy instituted by Christ, he comes to confess his sins, his actions are parts of the actual sacrament. These are completed and perfected by the words of absolution, pronounced by the minister in the name of Christ.

Thus the penitent experiences the mercy of God in his life. He proclaims that mercy and, together with the priest, celebrates the liturgy of the Church which is being perpetually renewed.

IV The Celebration of the Sacrament of Penance

12 The place of celebration
The sacrament of penance is administered in such places as are appointed in the church's law.

13 The time of celebration
The reconciliation of penitents can be celebrated at any time and on any day, but it is proper that the faithful should know the day and the hour at which the priest is present for the exercise of this ministry. The faithful should be encouraged to get into the

habit of going to confession at times which have already been arranged, and not during the celebration of mass.[44]

Lent is the most suitable time for the celebration of the sacrament of penance, because on Ash Wednesday the people of God are called upon to 'repent and believe the gospel'. It is desirable that several penitential services should take place during Lent, so that all the faithful may have an opportunity to be reconciled to God and to their fellow men, and to celebrate the paschal mystery during the Easter triduum renewed in mind and heart.

14 Liturgical vestments
The liturgical vestments to be worn for penitential services are to be such as are prescribed by the local ordinary.

A The service of reconciliation for individual penitents

15 Preparation of priest and penitent
Priest and penitent should prepare themselves for this sacrament by prayer. The priest calls upon the Holy Spirit for light and love. The penitent thinks over his life in the light of Christ's example and commandments, and begs God to take away his sins.

16 Reception of the penitent
The priest welcomes the penitent in friendly fashion, and may join the penitent in making the sign of the cross, as the penitent says: 'In the name of the Father and of the Son and of the Holy Spirit, Amen.' The priest then invites the penitent to put his trust in God. If the penitent is unknown to the confessor, he should explain his circumstances to the priest, and any difficulties he may have in leading a Christian life, and whatever else may be of use to the priest as a help in the administration of the sacrament. He should also tell the priest when he last went to confession.

17 Reading of the word of God
The priest or the penitent may now read a passage from scripture, which the latter may do when preparing for the celebration of the sacrament. The word of God is a help for the penitent in examining his conscience, and is at the same time a call to conversion and to trust in God's mercy.

18 Confession of sins and acceptance of penance
The penitent then confesses his sins, beginning, if this is customary

with a form of general confession, e.g. the I confess. If necessary the priest will help him to make a complete confession. He will exhort the penitent to sincere repentance for his offences against God. He will give him any counsel that may be useful for beginning a new life, and if necessary instruct him in the duties of the Christian life.

If the penitent has caused damage or scandal, the priest persuades him to make suitable reparation.

The priest then imposes a penance, which is not to be thought of simply as an expiation for past sins, but as a help in starting a new life and a remedy for human weakness. It should correspond as far as possible to the nature and gravity of the sins committed. It may take the form of prayer, or self-denial, but especially the service of others, so as to bring out the fact that both sin and its forgiveness have a social dimension.

19 The penitent's prayer and the priest's absolution

The penitent expresses his contrition and purpose of amendment in a prayer asking forgiveness of God the Father. This prayer should use some words of holy scripture.

When the penitent has said his prayer, the priest raises his hands over the penitent's head, or the right hand alone, and says the words of absolution, of which the essential part is: 'I absolve you from your sins in the name of the Father and of the Son and of the Holy Spirit.' While he is saying these words, he makes the sign of the cross over the penitent. The form of absolution (see 46) indicates that the reconciliation of the penitent comes from the mercy of the Father. It also shows the connection between the reconciliation of the sinner and the paschal mystery of Christ, and the part that the Holy Spirit plays in the forgiveness of sins. The ecclesial aspect of the sacrament is brought out by the fact that reconciliation is asked of, and granted by, the ministry of the church.

20 Thanksgiving and dismissal

The penitent's sins are now forgiven, and he gives thanks to God for his mercy with a brief invocation taken from the scriptures. The priest tells him to go in peace.

The penitent perseveres in his conversion, and expresses it by a life reformed according to the gospel of Christ, and more and more imbued with the love of God, for 'love covers over many a sin' (I Peter 4: 8).

21 If the pastoral situation demands it the priest may shorten or omit certain parts of the rite, apart from the following: confession of sins and acceptance of penance, exhortation to contrition (**44**), the form of absolution and the dismissal.

In danger of death it is sufficient for the priest to use only the form of absolution: 'I absolve you from your sins in the name of the Father and of the Son and of the Holy Spirit.'

B The Reconciliation of a group of penitents with individual confession and absolution

22 When a group of penitents is gathered together to receive the sacrament of reconciliation, it is fitting that they be prepared in the first place by a celebration of the word of God.

The service may also be attended by those who will go to confession on some other occasion.

A community celebration brings out the ecclesial nature of penance. All the faithful hear the word of God together, and they are all invited to change their lives by God's mercy, which is proclaimed in the readings. At the same time, they have an opportunity to reflect on whether or not their present life is in conformity with what they are told in the word of God, and they help each other with their prayers. When each one has confessed his sins and received absolution, all praise God together for his wonderful goodness towards the people he has made his own through the blood of his Son.

There should be a number of priests present, stationed in suitable places, for the absolution of all who wish to go to confession.

23 Introduction to the service

The congregation sing some suitable hymn or chant. The priest greets them, and he, or another minister, explains briefly what is about to take place. He invites the congregation to pray after a short period of silence.

24 The service of the word

The sacrament of penance should begin with the penitents listening to the word of God, which calls us to true and sincere repentance.

One or more readings may be chosen. If there are more than one, congregational singing or silence takes place between the readings. In this way the word of God is more deeply assimilated and the people are able to respond to it in their hearts. If there is only one lesson, it should be taken from the gospel.

The readings chosen should be concerned with:

a the voice of God calling men to a change of heart, and a greater conformity with Christ.

b the mystery of reconciliation, through the death and resurrection of Christ and the gift of the Holy Spirit.

c God's judgment of the good and the evil in men's lives. This is a help for the congregation in their examination of conscience.

25 The homily, taking its subject matter from the scripture texts, should aim at helping the congregation to examine their consciences, and turn away from their sins to God. The faithful are to be reminded that sin is committed not only against God but against the community, against their fellow men, and against themselves. The following should be brought to mind:

a God's infinite mercy, which is greater than all our sins. God is always calling us back to himself.

b The need for interior repentance. By its means we become disposed even to make reparation for the wrongdoing of sin.

c The social aspect of grace and sin, by which every act of the individual in some way has its repercussions on the whole body of the church.

d Satisfaction for sin, which gains its efficacy from the satisfaction that Christ has made for our sins. This requires not only that we do works of penance, but works which show a real charity towards God and our fellow men.

26 After the homily, there is to be a sufficient time for silence in which the congregation may examine their consciences and arouse in their hearts true sorrow for their sins. If it is deemed suitable, the priest or deacon may help the congregation with suggestions, or a prayer in the form of a litany may be recited.

The examination of conscience may take the place of the homily, for reasons of convenience, but in this case the scripture readings must clearly be seen as the point of departure for the examination of conscience.

27 The rite of reconciliation
The deacon or another minister calls upon the congregation to

kneel or bow their heads, and say together a form of general confession (e.g. the I confess). They remain standing for the litanic prayer or a suitable hymn or chant, by which they express their contrition and their trust in God's mercy. This is always followed by the Lord's prayer.

28 The priests then go to the various places where they will hear confessions. Those who wish to go to confession now do so and the priests absolve them, using the form for reconciling individual penitents.

29 The priests return to the sanctuary when all the confessions have been heard. The chief celebrant calls upon the congregation to join in an act of thanksgiving, which may take the form of a hymn or psalm or a form of litany. The concluding prayer is then said, in praise of God for the great love with which he has loved us.

30 Dismissal
The priest blesses the people, and the deacon dismisses them.

C The Reconciliation of a group of penitents with general confession and absolution

31 The rules for general absolution
The integral confession of the individual penitent, followed by absolution, remains the only normal way in which the faithful are reconciled to God and the church. Only cases of physical or moral impossibility constitute an exception to this rule.

There are, however, certain cases in which it is not only lawful but necessary to give absolution to a group of penitents without each one individually having previously been to confession.

Apart from the case of danger of death, it is lawful to absolve a group of penitents sacramentally who have made a general confession and have been called to true repentance, in cases of grave necessity where there is a large number of penitents and an insufficient number of priests to hear individual confessions within a reasonable time, with the consequence that if the penitents were not absolved they would, through no fault of their own, be deprived of sacramental grace, or even obliged to forgo holy communion for some length of time. This can happen especially in mission territories, but it can also happen in other places, and indeed with groups of people where the same need is present. The fact that there is a large number of people present is not sufficient reason in itself (as, for instance, during pilgrimages and festivals), as long as an adequate supply of confessors can be obtained to hear their confessions.[45]

32 The decision on the fact whether these conditions are realised in any given case, and therefore on the lawfulness of giving general sacramental absolution, is reserved to the bishop of the diocese, in agreement with other members of the episcopal conference.

Apart from the cases laid down by the bishop of the diocese, a priest must always have recourse as far as possible in any other case of grave necessity to the local ordinary for permission to give general sacramental absolution. He must inform the same ordinary of the reasons for his request, and must notify him as soon as possible when the absolution is given.[46]

33 It is required of the faithful who wish to avail themselves of general absolution that they be properly disposed. They must be sorry for all the sins they have committed. They must resolve to avoid sin in the future, and they must be resolved to make reparation for any scandal they may have caused or any damage they may have done. They must also resolve to go to confession in due course in order to confess those grave sins which they cannot confess during the penitential service. Priests must remind the faithful of all these conditions, which are required for the validity of the sacrament.[47]

34 Those who receive general absolution must go to confession privately before receiving a second general absolution, unless they are unable to do so for some just cause. Unless it is morally impossible, they must certainly go to confession within a year. The law still applies to them regarding the duty of every catholic to confess to a priest at least all his grave sins, not previously confessed privately, once a year.[48]

35 The rite of general absolution
When a group of penitents is to be reconciled with general confession and absolution, in those cases envisaged in the law, the rite is the same as for the reconciliation of a group of penitents with individual confession and communion, apart from the following:

a After or during the homily, the faithful are to be reminded that if they wish to receive general absolution they must be properly disposed. That is to say, they must be sorry for the sins they have committed, they must resolve to avoid sin in the future, and be prepared to make restitution for any scandal or damage they may have caused. Moreover, they must be resolved to confess all the grave sins they cannot confess during this service, in private confession in due course.[49] They undertake also to do whatever penance is imposed on them and they may add to the penance if they wish.

b The deacon or another minister, or the priest himself, then calls upon the penitents who wish to receive absolution to make some sign of their intention to do so, e.g. by kneeling or bowing the head or performing some other gesture as laid down by the episcopal conferences. They say together a form of general confession, e.g. the I confess, which may be followed by a prayer in litany form or penitential hymn or psalm. The Lord's prayer is used as a conclusion, as in **27**, above.

c The priest then says the prayers which call upon the grace of the Holy Spirit for the forgiveness of sins, and proclaim the victory of Christ's death and resurrection over sin. He then gives sacramental absolution to the penitents.

d The thanksgiving follows, as in **29**. The concluding prayer is omitted. The priest blesses the congregation and dismisses them.

V Penitential Services

36 Their character and structure

Penitential services are assemblies at which the people of God can hear the word of God calling them to repentance and renewal, and proclaiming our deliverance from sin through the death and resurrection of Christ. They are structured in the same way as is customary for celebrations of the word of God,[50] and in the manner laid down in the Service for the Reconciliation of a group of penitents.

It is appropriate that after the introductory rite (singing, greeting and prayer) one or more lessons from holy scripture be read. If more than one lesson is read, there should be singing or a time of silence observed between the lessons. The homily is given after the readings, and it draws upon them in order to instruct the congregation. Other readings may be added, before or after the lessons from scripture, from patristic authors or others of a type that will be useful to the congregation in achieving true contrition and a change of heart.

After the homily and meditation on the word of God, the congregation should pray together, using a litanic prayer or some other method that will enable them to share in the service more fully. The Lord's prayer is always to be used as a conclusion, calling on God our Father to 'forgive us our trespasses as we forgive those who trespass against us . . . and deliver us from evil'. The priest or other presiding minister finishes with a prayer and dismisses the congregation.

37 Usefulness and importance
Care must be taken that, in the minds of the faithful, these services should not be confused with the celebration of the sacrament of penance itself.[51] These services are most useful in helping the faithful to purify their hearts and turn their lives towards God.[52]

Penitential services are especially useful for:
—encouraging a spirit of repentance in the Christian community.
—helping the faithful in preparing for the confession that they will make individually at a later date.
—educating children in the gradual formation of conscience, and in their awareness of sin in human life and of deliverance from sin through Christ.
—helping catechumens during the time of their conversion.

Penitential services are extremely useful even when no priest is present to give sacramental absolution, as a help to achieving contrition motivated by the perfect love of God. The faithful can thus obtain grace through their desire for sacramental penance at some future time.[53]

VI Adaptations of the Rite for different localities

Adaptations to be made by episcopal conferences.

38 It belongs to the episcopal conferences, when they draw up rituals for local use, to adapt the penitential rites of this Order to the needs of their region, so that after confirmation by the Apostolic See they may be used in their territories. Episcopal conferences will therefore:

a Lay down the laws governing the discipline of the sacrament of penance, especially in regard to the priest's ministry and the reservation of certain sins.

b Define precisely what places are suitable for the celebration penance, and by what signs the faithful are to show their desire for general absolution (see 35 above).

c Prepare versions of the texts that will be truly adapted to every kind of congregation and to their mentality and language, and compose new texts for the prayers of the faithful and ministers, with the exception of the sacramental formula which must remain unchanged.

39 The responsibility of bishops

It belongs to the bishop:

a To supervise the discipline of penance in his diocese[54] and apply any appropriate changes in the rites of penance that have been proposed by the episcopal conference.

b To decide when it is lawful for general sacramental absolution to be given. The bishop does this in accordance with the conditions laid down by the Holy See, and in agreement with the other members of the episcopal conference.[55]

40 Adaptations to be made by the minister

It is the duty of priests, especially of parish priests:

a to adapt the rite of the service of reconciliation, whether for individuals or groups, to the condition and circumstances of the penitents. The essential structure and integral formula of absolution are to remain unchanged, but for pastoral reasons some parts of the services may be omitted or amplified, and alternative readings and prayers may be selected. Within the norms laid down by the episcopal conference, a priest may chose whatever place is best suited for the service with a view to the maximum spiritual benefit of the congregation.

b to arrange and prepare penitential services on different occasions during the year, especially during Lent, with the help of the laity, so that the texts selected and the lay-out of the service may be really suitable for the special needs and circumstances of the congregation (e.g. children, the sick, etc.).

c In the case of grave necessity, unforeseen by the bishop of the diocese, and if recourse to the bishop is not possible, it is for the priest to decide whether he shall give sacramental absolution after general confession. In such a case, the priest must inform the bishop as soon as possible of the grave necessity in question, and of the fact that he has given the absolution.

NOTES

1 See II Cor. 5: 18 ff., Col. 1: 20.
2 See John 8: 34–36.
3 I Peter 2: 9.
4 Luke 15.
5 Luke 5: 20, 27–32; 7, 48.
6 See Matt. 9: 2–8.
7 See Rom. 4: 25.
8 See Roman Missal, Eucharistic Prayer III.
9 See Matt. 26: 28.
10 See John 20: 19–23.
11 See Luke 24: 47.
12 See Acts 3: 19, 26; 17, 30.
13 See Rom. 6: 4–10.
14 Roman Missal, Eucharistic Prayer III.
15 Roman Missal, Eucharistic Prayer II.
16 See Council of Trent, Session XIV, 'On the Sacrament of Penance', Ch. 1: DENZ.-SCHÖN. 1668 and 1670; can. 1: DENZ.-SCHÖN. 1701.
17 St Ambrose, Letters 41, 12: PL 16, 1116.
18 See Rev. 19: 7.
19 See Eph. 1: 22–23; Vatican Council II, Const. *Lumen gentium*, n. 7: AAS 57 (1965), pp. 9–11.
20 Vatican Council II, Const. *Lumen gentium*, n. 8: *ibid.*, p. 12. Trans. Rev. Avery Dulles, S.J. in *The Documents of Vatican II*, Geoffrey Chapman, London 1970.
21 See I Peter 4: 13.
22 See I Peter 4: 8.
23 See Council of Trent, Session XIV, 'On the Sacrament of Penance'; DENZ.-SCHÖN. 1638, 1740, 1743; Sacred Congregation of Rites, Instr. *Eucharisticum mysterium*, 25 May 1967, n. 35: AAS 59 (1967), pp. 560–1; Roman Missal, *Institutio generalis*, nn. 29, 30, 56 a.b.g.
24 Vatican Council II, Const. *Lumen gentium*, n. 11: AAS 57 (1965), pp. 15–16.
25 PAUL VI, Apost. Const. *Paenitemini*, 17 February 1966: AAS 58 (1966), p. 179; cf. Vatican Council II, Const. *Lumen gentium*, n. 11: AAS 57 (1965), pp. 15–16.
26 See Gal. 2: 20; Eph. 5, 25.
27 See Tit. 3: 6.

28 PAUL VI, Apost. Const. *Indulgentiarum doctrina*, 1 January 1967, n. 4 AAS 59 (1967), p. 9; cf. PIUS XII, Encyclical letter *Mystici Corporis*, 29 June 1943: AAS 35 (1943), p. 213.

29 See Council of Trent, Session XIV, 'On the Sacrament of Penance', Ch. 1: DENZ.-SCHÖN. 1673–1675.

30 *Ibid.*, Ch. 4: DENZ.-SCHÖN, 1676.

31 PAUL VI, Apost. Const. *Paenitemini*, 17 February 1966: AAS 58 (1966), p. 179.

32 See Council of Trent, Session XIV, 'On the Sacrament of Penance', Ch. 5: DENZ.-SCHÖN, 1679.

33 See Council of Trent, Session XIV, 'On the Sacrament of Penance', Ch. 8: DENZ.-SCHÖN. 1690–1692; PAUL VI, Apost. Const. *Indulgentiarum doctrina*, 1 January 1967, nn. 2–3: AAS 59 (1967), pp. 6–8.

34 See Tit. 3: 4–5.

35 See Luke 15: 7, 10, 32.

36 See Council of Trent, Session XIV, 'On the Sacrament of Penance', can. 7–8: DENZ.-SCHÖN. 1707–1708.

37 See II Cor. 4: 10.

38 See Gal. 4: 31.

39 See Matt. 18: 18; John 20: 23.

40 See Vatican Council II, Const. *Lumen gentium*, n. 26: AAS 57 (1965), pp. 31–2.

41 See Phil. 1: 9–10.

42 See Sacred Congregation for the Doctrine of the Faith, *Normae pastorales circa absolutionem sacramentalem generali modo impertiendam*, 16 June 1972, n. XII: AAS 64 (1972), p. 514.

43 See Vatican Council II, Const. *Sacrosanctum Concilium*, n. 7: AAS 56 (1964), pp. 100–1.

44 See Sacred Congregation of Rites, Instr. *Eucharisticum mysterium*, 25 May 1967, n. 35; AAS 59 (1967), pp. 560–1.

45 Sacred Congregation for the Doctrine of the Faith, *Normae pastorales circa absolutionem sacramentalem generali modo impertiendam*, 16 June 1972, n. III: AAS 64 (1972), p. 511.

46 *Ibid.*, n. V: l.c., p. 512.

47 *Ibid.*, nn. VI and XI: l.c., pp. 512, 514.

48 *Ibid.*, nn. VII and VIII: l.c., pp. 512–13.

49 See *ibid.*, n. VI, p. 512.

50 See Sacred Congregation of Rites, Instr. *Inter Oecumenici*, 26 September 1964, nn. 37–9: AAS 56 (1964), pp. 110–11.

51 See Sacred Congregation for the Doctrine of the Faith, *Normae pastorales circa absolutionem sacramentalem generali modo impertiendam*, 16 June 1972, n. X: AAS 64 (1972), pp. 513–14.

52 *Ibid.*

53 See Council of Trent, Session XIV, 'On the Sacrament of Penance', Ch. 5: DENZ.-SCHÖN. 1677.

54 See Vatican Council II, Const. *Lumen gentium*, n. 26: AAS 57 (1965), pp. 31–2.

55 See Sacred Congregation for the Doctrine of the Faith, *Normae pastorales circa absolutionem sacramentalem generali modo impertiendam*, n. V: AAS 64 (1972), p. 512.

I The Reconciliation of individual Penitents

41 Reception of the penitent
When the penitent comes to confess his sins, the priest welcomes him with a friendly greeting.

42 The penitent makes the sign of the cross, and the priest may do the same, saying: In the name of the Father, and of the Son, and of the Holy Spirit. Amen.

The priest tells the penitent to put his trust in God, using these or similar words:

—May God who lights up our hearts, help you to acknowledge your sins and reveal to you his mercy.

The penitent answers: Amen.

(Other texts will be found 67–71).

43 Reading of the Word of God (optional)
The priest may read or recite from memory some text from scripture concerning the mercy of God and his call to repentance. (Texts will be found 72–84.)

44 Confession of sins and satisfaction
If it is customary, the penitent says the I confess, and then confesses his sins.

If necessary, the priest helps the penitent to make a full confession. He offers appropriate counsel, and helps the penitent to achieve true contrition, reminding him that the sacrament of penance is a re-enactment of the paschal mystery, in which a Christian dies and rises again with Christ. The priest then gives the penitent his penance, which he accepts in order to make satisfaction for his sins and to amend his life.

The priest must be careful to adapt himself in every way to the penitent's condition, in what he says, and in the kind of counselling he gives.

45 The penitent's prayer
The priest then invites the penitent to manifest his contrition, which he may do in these or similar words:

My God, I repent with all my heart and I am sorry for all the

wrong I have done, and the good I have failed to do, because by
my sins I have offended you, who are the supreme good, and
more to be loved than anything else.

With the help of your grace I am resolved to do penance, to
sin no more, and to avoid the occasions of sin.

Through the merits of the passion of our Saviour Jesus Christ,
have mercy on me, Lord.

(Other texts will be found 85–92.)

46 The absolution
The priest then stretches out both hands (or the right hand
alone) over the penitent's head, and says:

God, the Father of all mercy, has reconciled the world to himself through the death and resurrection of his Son. He has sent
the Holy Spirit for the forgiveness of sins. Through the ministry
of the church may he grant you pardon and peace. I absolve you
from your sins in the name of the Father and of the Son ✠ and
of the Holy Spirit.

The penitent answers: Amen.

47 Thanksgiving and dismissal
After the absolution the priest says:

Let us give thanks to the Lord for he is good.

The penitent answers:

For his love endures for ever.

The priest concludes:

The Lord has forgiven you your sins. Go in peace.

(Other texts 93.)

II *The Reconciliation of a group of Penitents, with*
individual Confession and Absolution

48 The congregation sing a suitable psalm or hymn or antiphon
as the priest enters, e.g.

—Hear us, O Lord, in your mercy. Look down on us Lord, in
your great kindness.

or:

—Let us approach the throne of grace with confidence, that
we may obtain mercy, grace and help in our need.

49 The greeting

—The grace and peace of God our Father and of Jesus Christ our Saviour be with you.

R. And also with you.

or:

—The grace and peace of God our Father and of Jesus Christ be with us. He has washed away our sins in his blood.

R. To him be glory for ever, Amen.

(Other alternative texts, **94–96**.)

The priest or other minister now speaks to the congregation, briefly explaining the importance and meaning of the service, and the manner in which it is to be performed.

50 The priest invites the congregation to prayer, using the following, or similar words.

—My brothers and sisters, let us pray that God, who has called us to turn away from sin, may grant us the grace of true and fruitful repentance.

A period of silent prayer follows, after which the priest says:

—Lord hear us as we pray to you, and forgive us as we confess our sins. Grant us pardon and peace, through Christ our Lord. Amen.

or:

—May your Holy Spirit be in our midst, O Lord, to wash us in the pure water of repentance, and to make of us a living sacrifice. With the life of the Spirit within us, may we praise you in every place for your mercy and your glory. Through Christ our Lord, Amen.

(Other alternative texts, **97–100**.)

51 Celebration of God's Word

The service of the Word now follows. If several lessons are read, they should be interspersed with psalms or periods of silence, so that the people may meditate on the word of God. If only one lesson is read, it should be a passage from the gospel.

1 Theme: 'Love is the fulfilment of the law'

First reading Deut. 5: 1–3, 6–7, 11–12, 16–21a; 6: 4–6:
'You shall love the Lord your God with all your heart.'

Responsorial psalm Baruch 1: 15–22.

R. (3: 2): 'Listen and have pity Lord, for we have sinned in your sight.'

Second reading Eph. 5: 1–14: 'Follow Christ by loving as he loved you.'

Verse John 8: 12: 'I am the light of the world; anyone who follows me will not be walking in the dark.'

Gospel Matt 22: 34–40: 'On these two commandments hang the whole law, and the prophets also.'

or John 13: 34–35; 15: 10–13: 'I give you a new commandment.'

2 Theme: 'Your mind must be renewed by a spiritual revolution'

First reading Is. 1: 10–18: 'Cease to do evil, learn to do good.'

Responsorial psalm Ps. 50.

R. v. 17: 'My sacrifice is this broken spirit.'

Second reading Eph. 4: 23–32: 'Your mind must be renewed by a spiritual revolution.'

Verse Matt 11: 28: 'Come to me, all you who labour and are overburdened, and I will give you rest.'

Gospel Matt 5: 1–12: 'Happy are the poor in spirit.'

(Other texts will be found 101–201.)

52 Homily
This is based on the readings, and aims to help the penitents to examine their consciences and amend their lives.

53 Examination of conscience
A time of silence is now observed so that the faithful may be able to examine their consciences and be truly contrite for their sins. The priest, deacon, or some other minister, can help with appropriate suggestions, or some prayer of a litanic kind that is suitable to the age and condition of the congregation.

The rite of reconciliation

54 The general confession of sins
The deacon or another minister invites the congregation to kneel or bow their heads, and all say together a form of general confession, e.g. the I confess. Then all stand and recite one of the

following litanies, or sing a suitable hymn. The Lord's prayer is always to be included at the end.

First litany

Deacon or minister: My brother and sisters, confess your sins and pray for each other that you may be saved.

All: I confess to almighty God, and to you, my brothers and sisters, that I have sinned through my own fault (they strike their breast) in my thoughts and in my words, in what I have done and in what I have failed to do; and I ask blessed Mary, ever virgin, all the angels and saints and you, my brothers and sisters, to pray for me to the Lord our God.

Deacon or minister:

—Let us pray: Purify our hearts, Lord, as we confess our sins. Forgive us for the faults of which we accuse ourselves. Heal our wounds and pardon us who are guilty.

—Grant us the grace of true repentance.

R. Lord, hear us.

—Forgive your servants the sins of the past.

R. Lord, hear us.

—May your children who have strayed from the church through sin, be brought back in safety through your forgiveness.

R. Lord, hear us.

—Cleanse us from all the strains of sin, that we may be clothed anew in the white garment of baptism.

R. Lord, hear us.

—To those of us who now return to Holy Communion, renew the hope of eternal glory.

R. Lord, hear us.

—May we remain faithful to your sacraments from this day forward, and never depart from you, O Lord.

R. Lord, hear us.

—Renewed in your love, may we be witnesses of that same love among our fellow men.

R. Lord, hear us.

—May we persevere in keeping your commandments and obtain everlasting life.

R. Lord, hear us.

—Let us now pray to God our Father in the words that Christ taught us, so that He may forgive us our sins and deliver us from all evil. Our Father ... (said by all).

The priest concludes:
—Uphold us, Lord, with your grace, as we confess ourselves to be sinners in your church. May we be freed from all sin through her ministry, and give you thanks with a pure heart, through Christ our Lord. Amen.

Second litany

Deacon or minister: Remembering the kindness of God our Father, let us confess our sins so that we may obtain mercy.
All: I confess . . . (as before).
Deacon: Let us humbly pray to Christ our Saviour, who is our just advocate with the Father.
May he forgive us our sins and purify us from all evil.
—You were sent to proclaim the good news to the poor, and to heal the contrite of heart.
R. Lord, be merciful to me, a sinner (or: Lord, have mercy).
—You came, not to call the just, but sinners.
R. Lord. . . .
—You forgave much to the one who loved you greatly.
R. Lord. . . .
—You did not hesitate to mix with publicans and sinners.
R. Lord. . . .
—On your own shoulders, you carried the lost sheep back to the fold.
R. Lord. . . .
—You did not condemn the adulteress, but let her go in peace.
R. Lord. . . .
—You called Zacchaeus the tax gatherer to conversion and a new way of life.
R. Lord. . . .
—You promised paradise to the penitent thief.
R. Lord. . . .
—Enthroned at the Father's right hand, you are always interceding for us.
—Let us together now pray to the Father as Christ commanded us. As we forgive one another, may we also be forgiven by Him.
R. Our Father. . . .
—Lord God, you have helped us to overcome our weakness. May our lives bear witness to the saving power that has healed us, and may we rejoice in it always, through Christ our Lord. Amen.
(Other alternative texts, 202–205.)

55   The penitents then go to confession individually, and each receives his penance and is absolved. When the priest has heard the penitent's confession, and after suitable words of counsel (if he so wishes), he omits the usual form for the reconciliation of individual penitents, and, holding both hands (or only the right hand) over the penitent's head, he pronounces the absolution:

God, the Father of all mercy, has reconciled the world to himself through the death and resurrection of his Son. He has sent the Holy Spirit for the forgiveness of sins. Through the ministry of the church may he grant you pardon and peace. I absolve you from your sins in the name of the Father and of the Son ✠ and of the Holy Spirit.

The penitent answers: Amen.

56   Praise of God's mercy

When all the confessions are finished, the celebrant and the other priests invite the congregation to give thanks. He exhorts them to good works, by which the grace of repentance will be manifested in the life of each individual and of the whole community. A hymn or psalm may be sung, or a litany in praise of God's power and mercy. The Magnificat may also be used, or Ps. 135 (136), vv. 1–9, 13–14, 16, 25–26.

(Other suitable texts will be found in **206**.)

57   Concluding prayer of thanksgiving

—Almighty and merciful God, you have renewed mankind, and made him more wonderful than he was when you first created him. You never abandon the sinner, but pursue him always with your fatherly love. You sent your Son into the world so that, by his passion, he might destroy sin and death, and bring us back to life and joy through his resurrection. You have sent the Holy Spirit into our hearts so that we might become your sons and heirs. With your saving sacraments you continue to give us new life so that we may be freed from the slavery of sin and transformed day by day into the image of your beloved Son. We give you thanks for your wonderful mercy. With voice and heart and deed, we praise you with the whole church. Through Jesus Christ, in the Holy Spirit, glory to you now and forever, Amen.

or :

—Holy Father, you have fashioned us anew in the image of your Son. Grant that we who have received your mercy, may become witnesses of your love in the world. Through Christ our Lord. Amen.

(Other alternative texts, **207–211**.)

58 The blessing
—May the Lord turn your hearts towards the love of God and the fortitude of Christ.
All: Amen.
—That you may walk in newness of life and please God in all things.
All: Amen.
—And may almighty God bless you, the Father, the Son ✠ and the Holy Spirit.
All: Amen.

(Other alternative texts **212–214**.)

59 *Deacon:* The Lord has forgiven your sins. Go in peace.
R. Thanks be to God.

III The Reconciliation of a group of Penitents with general Confession and Absolution

60 The service is the same as the previous one, apart from the following changes.

After the homily, or at some point during the homily, the priest reminds those who wish to receive general absolution that they must have the right dispositions. Everyone must be sorry for the sins he has committed, and must be resolved to avoid committing them in the future. If any scandal or damage has been caused, he must make reparation. Everyone must undertake to confess, in due course, grave sins which cannot be confessed at this service. The minister enjoins upon everyone a certain penance, to which individuals may add whatever other penance they wish.

61 General confession
The deacon or some other minister, or the priest himself, invites the penitents who wish to receive general absolution to show their desire for it, e.g.

—Will those who wish to receive sacramental absolution now kneel and make the general confession.

or :

—Will those who wish to receive sacramental absolution now bow their heads and make the general confession.

(Other methods of showing their wish to receive absolution may be devised by the episcopal conferences.)

The penitents make their general confession (e.g. the I confess) and after this some suitable prayer in litany form or hymn may be sung (see 54 for the reconciliation of a group of penitents with individual confession and absolution). This is always concluded with the Our Father.

62 General absolution

The priest gives absolution with his hands stretched out over the penitents.

—God, our Father, does not desire the death of a sinner, but rather that he should turn from wickedness and live. May He who first loved us, and sent his Son into the world to save it, show you his mercy and give you peace. Amen.

—Our Lord Jesus Christ, was given up for our sins and rose again for our justification. He poured out the Holy Spirit on his apostles and gave them the power to forgive sins. May he through our ministry free you from sin, and fill you with the Holy Spirit. Amen.

—The Holy Spirit, the Advocate (through whom we have access to the Father) was given to us that our sins might be taken away, and may he purify your hearts and fill them with his radiance, so that you may declare his mighty deeds. He has called you from darkness into his wonderful light. Amen.

—I absolve you from your sins in the Name of the Father and of the Son ✠ and of the Holy Spirit. Amen.

or :

—God the Father of mercy has reconciled the world to himself through the death and resurrection of his Son. He has sent the Holy Spirit for the forgiveness of sins. Through the ministry of the church, may he grant you pardon and peace. I absolve you from your sins in the name of the Father and of the Son ✠ and of the Holy Spirit. *R*. Amen.

63 Thanksgiving and Conclusion

The priest invites all present to give thanks and proclaim the mercy of God. A suitable hymn or chant is then sung. The concluding prayer is omitted. The priest blesses the people and dismisses them, as in 58–59 for reconciliation with individual confession and absolution.

64 Shorter Form
In cases of necessity, the reconciliation of a group of penitents with general confession and absolution may be shortened. After a brief scripture reading and the admonition as in 60 the priest imposes a penance. They make their general confession, e.g. the I confess, and the priest gives absolution as in 62.

65 When there is danger of death, it is sufficient for the priest to give absolution which may be shortened thus:
—I absolve you from your sins in the name of the Father and of the Son ✠ and of the Holy Spirit. R. Amen.

66 The faithful who have been absolved from grave sins by general sacramental absolution, are bound to confess these in their next individual confession.

IV Texts for use in Services of Reconciliation

I For the reconciliation of a single penitent

Theme: Trusting in God

67 Come to the Lord, who says: 'I take pleasure, not in the death of a sinner, but in the turning back of a sinner who changes his ways to win life' (Ez. 33: 11).

68 May the Lord give you courage, for he says: 'I have come not to call the virtuous, but sinners to repentance' (Luke 5: 32).

69 May the grace of the Holy Spirit enlighten your heart and give you confidence to confess your sins, so that you may know the mercy of God.

70 May the Lord be in your heart so that you may confess your sins with true contrition.

71 If you have sinned, do not lose heart. We have an advocate with the Father, Jesus Christ, who is just. He is the sacrifice

that takes our sins away, and not only ours, but the whole world's (1 John 2: 1–2).

Short scripture readings:

72
Is. 53: 4–6
Let us look to Jesus, who suffered for our salvation and rose again for our justification.
'Ours were the sufferings he bore, ours the sorrows he carried. But we, we thought of him as someone punished, struck by God, and brought low. Yet he was pierced through for our faults, crushed for our sins. On him lies a punishment that brings us peace, and through his wounds we are healed. We had all gone astray like sheep, each taking his own way, and God burdened him with the sins of all of us.'

73
Ez. 11: 19–20
Let us listen to the Lord who says to us:
'I will give them a single heart, and I will put a new spirit in them. I will remove the heart of stone from their bodies and give them a heart of flesh instead, so that they will keep my laws and respect my observances and put them into practice. Then they shall be my people and I will be their God.'

74
Matt 6: 14–15
Let us listen to the Lord who says to us:
'If you forgive others their failings, your heavenly Father will forgive you yours. But if you do not forgive others, your Father will not forgive your failings either.'

75
Mark 1: 14–15
After John had been arrested, Jesus went into Galilee. There he proclaimed the Good News from God. 'The time has come,' he said, 'and the kingdom of heaven is close at hand. Repent, and believe the Good News.'

76
Luke 6: 31–38
Let us listen to the Lord who tells us:
'Treat others as you would like them to treat you. If you love

those who love you, what thanks can you expect? Even sinners love those who love them. And if you do good to those who do good to you, what thanks can you expect? For even sinners do that much. And if you lend to those from whom you hope to receive, what thanks can you expect? Even sinners lend to sinners and get back the same amount. Instead, love your enemies and do good, and lend without any hope of return. You will have a great reward, and you will be sons of the Most High, for he himself is kind to the ungrateful and the wicked.

Be compassionate as your Father is compassionate. Do not judge, and you will not be judged yourselves; grant pardon, and you will be pardoned. Give, and there will be gifts for you: a full measure, pressed down, shaken together, and running over, will be poured into your lap; because the amount you measure out is the amount you will be given back.'

77
Luke 15: 1–7
The tax collectors and sinners were all seeking the company of Jesus to hear what he had to say, and the Pharisees and the scribes complained. 'This man,' they said, 'welcomes sinners and eats with them.' So he spoke this parable to them.

'What man among you with a hundred sheep, losing one, would not leave the ninety-nine in the wilderness and go after the missing one till he found it? And when he found it, would he not joyfully take it on his shoulders and then when he got home, call together his friends and neighbours? "Rejoice with me," he would say, "I have found my sheep that was lost." In the same way, I tell you, there will be more rejoicing in heaven over one repentant sinner than over ninety-nine virtuous men who have no need of repentance.'

78
John 20: 19–23
'In the evening of that same day, the first day of the week, the doors were closed in the room where the disciples were, for fear of the Jews. Jesus came and stood among them. He said to them "Peace be with you", and showed them his hands and his side. The disciples were filled with joy when they saw the Lord, and he said to them again, "Peace be with you. As the Father sent me, so am I sending you." And saying this he breathed on them and said: "Receive the Holy Spirit. For those whose sins

you forgive, they are forgiven; for those whose sins you retain, they are retained." '

79
Rom. 5: 8–9
'What proves that God loves us is that Christ died for us while we were still sinners. Having died to make us righteous, is it likely that he would now fail to save us from God's anger?'

80
Eph. 5: 1–2
'Try, then, to imitate God, as children of his that he loves, and follow Christ by loving as he loved you, giving himself up in our place as a fragrant offering and a sacrifice to God.'

81
Col. 1: 12–14
'Let us give thanks to the Father who has made it possible for you to join the saints and with them to inherit the light. Because that is what he has done: he has taken us out of the power of darkness and created a place for us in the kingdom of the Son that he loves, and in him, we gain our freedom, the forgiveness of our sins.'

82
Col. 3. 8–10: 12–17
'Now you, of all people, must give all these things up: getting angry, being bad-tempered, spitefulness, abusive language and dirty talk; and never tell each other lies. You have stripped off your old behaviour with your old self, and you have put on a new self which will progress towards true knowledge the more it is renewed in the image of its creator.

'You are God's chosen race, his saints; he loves you, and you should be clothed in sincere compassion, in kindness and humility, gentleness and patience. Bear with one another; forgive each other as soon as a quarrel begins. The Lord has forgiven you; now you must do the same. Over all these clothes, to keep them together and complete them, put on love. And may the peace of Christ reign in your hearts, because it is for this that you were called together as parts of one body. Always be thankful.

'Let the message of Christ, in all its richness, find a home with you. Teach each other, and advise each other, in all wisdom. With gratitude in your hearts sing psalms and hymns and inspired songs to God; and never say or do anything except in the name of the Lord Jesus, giving thanks to God the Father through him.'

83
I John 1: 6–7, 9
'If we say that we are in union with God while we are living in darkness, we are lying because we are not living the truth. But if we live our lives in the light, as he is in the light, we are in union with one another, and the blood of Jesus, his Son, purifies us from all sin. If we acknowledge our sins, then God who is faithful and just will forgive our sins and purify us from everything that is wrong.'

84 The lessons in the service for a group of penitents, **101–201**, may also be used, and any other readings from scripture that priest or penitent may desire.

The prayer of the penitent

85 Remember your kindness, Lord, your love that you showed long ago. Do not remember the sins of my youth; but rather, with your love remember me (Ps 24 (25): 6–7).

86 Wash me clean of my guilt, O Lord, and purify me from my sin. For I am well aware of my faults, I have my sin constantly in mind (Ps 50 (51): 2–3).

87 Father, I have sinned against you. I am not worthy to be called your son. Be merciful to me, a sinner (Luke 15: 18; 18: 13).

88 Most merciful Father, as a repentant son I turn back to you and say, 'I have sinned against you and am no longer worthy to be called your son.' Jesus Christ, Saviour of the world, I beg you, like the penitent thief, 'Remember me when you come into your kingdom.' Holy Spirit, fount of love, I call upon you trustfully, 'Purify me, and grant that I may walk as a child of the light.'

89 Lord Jesus, you opened the eyes of the blind, you healed the sick. You forgave the woman taken in adultery, and after Peter had betrayed you, you strengthened him in love. Hear my prayer and forgive all my sins. Renew your love within me. Grant me to live in perfect unity with my fellow Christians, that I may declare your salvation to my fellow men.

90 Lord Jesus, you were a friend of sinners. By the mystery of your death and resurrection, deliver me from my sins. May your peace be active in my heart, that I may bring forth the fruits of charity, justice and truth.

91 Lord Jesus Christ, lamb of God who takes away the sin of the world, reconcile me to your Father through the grace of the Holy Spirit. Wash me in your blood from all guilt, and give me life that I may praise your glory.

92 Have mercy on me, O God, in your goodness. Turn away your face from my sins and blot out all my iniquities. Create a pure heart in me, O God, and renew your spirit within me.
or:
Lord Jesus, Son of God, be merciful to me, a sinner.

93 After the absolution, the celebrant may add the following in place of the thanksgiving and dismissal.
May the Passion of our Lord Jesus Christ, the intercession of the blessed Virgin Mary, and of all the Saints, whatever good you do, and whatever evil you suffer, be a remedy for your sins, and obtain for you grace, and the reward of eternal life. Go in peace.
or:
The Lord has set you free from sin. May he keep you safe in his heavenly kingdom. To him be glory for ever. Amen.
or:
Happy the man whose fault is forgiven, whose sin is blotted out. Rejoice and be glad in the Lord, and go in peace.
or:
Go in peace, and tell the world of God's wonders, for he has made you whole.

II The Reconciliation of a group of Penitents

The Greeting

94 May grace, mercy and peace be with you from God the Father and from Jesus Christ, his Son, in truth and love.

95 My brothers and sisters, may God open your hearts to his law, and make peace among you. May he grant your prayers and reconcile you to himself. Amen.

96 May grace and peace be with you, from God our Father and Our Lord Jesus Christ who gave himself for our sins.
R. Glory be to God for ever. Amen.
Other greetings from the beginning of the Mass may be used.

Prayers to be said over the congregation

97 Absolve us, O Lord, from all our sins, so that we may serve you with a free mind, through Christ Our Lord. Amen.

98 Lord our God, we confess that we have sinned against you. Look mercifully upon us who have offended you, since you never turn away from us, but always graciously accept our penance. Grant that we may celebrate the sacraments of your mercy, and after a life chastened by penitence we may enjoy eternal blessedness, through Christ our Lord. Amen.

99 Almighty and merciful God, you have gathered us together in the name of your Son, so that we might obtain mercy and the help of your grace. Open our eyes to the evil we have done. Touch our hearts that we may turn to you in sincerity. Where sin has caused division among us, may your love bring us together. Where our weakness has defiled us, may your power bring healing and strength. What death has destroyed in us, may your Spirit bring back to life. With your love renewed in us, may the image of your Son be visible to all men in our lives. May the light of Christ shine on the face of your glorious church, so that the whole world may know your Son whom you sent to us, Jesus Christ our Lord. Amen.

100 Father of mercy and God of all consolation, you have said that you wish for the conversion of the sinner, and not for his death. Come to the aid of your people that they may return to you and live. Help us, as we listen to your words, so that we may be able to confess our sins, and give you thanks for your pardon. Let us grow in every way, doing the truth in charity, into the full stature of Christ your Son who lives and reigns for ever. Amen.

Bible readings

These readings have been selected as suitable both for the pastor and the congregation, but others may be chosen if considered more appropriate.

Old Testament readings

101 Gen. 3: 1–19: 'She took some of its fruit and ate it.'

102 Gen. 4: 1–15: 'Cain set on his brother Abel and killed him.'

103 Gen. 18: 17–33: 'I will not destroy it,' he replied, 'for the sake of ten.'

104 Ex. 17: 1–7: 'They put Yahweh to the test by saying: Is Yahweh with us or not?'

105 Ex. 20: 1–21: 'I am Yahweh your God . . . you shall have no gods except me.'

106 Deut. 6: 4–9: 'You shall love Yahweh your God with all your heart.'

107 Deut. 9: 7–19: 'They have been quick to leave the way I marked out for them.'

108 Deut. 30: 15–20: 'See, today I set before you life and prosperity, death and disaster.'

109 II Sam. 12: 1–9, 13: 'David said to Nathan: I have sinned against Yahweh. Then Nathan said to David: Yahweh for his part forgives your sin, you are not to die.'

110 Neh. 9: 1–20: 'The Israelites, in sackcloth and with dust on their heads, assembled for a fast.'

111 Wis. 1: 1–16: 'Wisdom will never make its way into a crafty soul, nor stay in a body that is in debt to sin.'

112 Wis. 5: 1–16: 'The hope of the godless is like chaff carried on the wind . . . but the virtuous live for ever.'

113 Sir. 28: 1–7: 'Forgive your neighbour the hurt he does you, and when you pray, your sins will be forgiven.'

114 Is. 1: 2–6, 15–18: 'I reared sons, I brought them up, but they have rebelled against me.'

115 Is. 5: 1–7: 'My friend had a vineyard. . . . He expected it to yield grapes, but sour grapes were all that it gave.'

116 Is. 43: 22–28: 'It is I, I it is, who must blot out everything.'

117 Is. 53: 1–12: 'Yahweh burdened him with the sins of all of us.'

118 Is. 55: 1–11: 'Let the wicked man abandon his way, the evil man his thoughts. Let him turn back to Yahweh who will take pity on him, to our God who is rich in forgiving.'

119 Is. 58: 1–11: 'If you give your bread to the hungry, and relief to the oppressed, your light will rise in the darkness, and your shadows become like noon.'

120 Is. 59: 1–4, 9–15: 'Your iniquities have made a gulf between you and your God.'

121 Jer. 2: 1–13: 'My people have committed a double crime. They have abandoned me, the fountain of living water, only to dig cisterns for themselves, leaky cisterns that hold no water.'

122 Jer. 7: 21–26: 'Listen to my voice, then I will be your God, and you shall be my people.'

123 Ez. 11: 14–21: 'I will remove the heart of stone from their bodies, and give them a heart of flesh instead.'

124 Ez. 18: 20–32: 'If the wicked man renounces all the sins he has committed . . . he will certainly live, he will not die.'

125 Ez. 36: 23–28: 'I shall pour clean water over you . . . I shall put a new spirit in you, and make you keep my laws.'

126 Hos. 2: 16–25: 'I will make a treaty on her behalf.'

127 Hos. 11: 1–11: 'I took them in my arms, yet they have not understood that I was the one looking after them.'

128 Hos. 14: 2–10: 'Israel, come back to Yahweh your God.'

129 Joel 2: 12–19: 'Come back to me with all your heart.'

130 Mic. 6: 1–15: 'To act justly, to love tenderly and to walk humbly with your God.'

131 Mic. 7: 2–7, 18–20: 'Once more have pity on us, tread down our faults, to the bottom of the sea throw all our sins.'

132 Zec. 1: 1–6: 'Return to me, and I will return to you.'

Responsorial Psalms

133 Ps. 12 (13).
   R. v. 5: 'But I for my part rely on your love.'

134 Ps. 24 (25).
   R. v. 16: 'Turn to me, take pity on me.'

135 Ps 30 (31).
   R. v. 5–6: 'You have redeemed me, God of truth.'

136 Ps. 31 (32).
   R. v. 5: 'You have pardoned my sin.'

137 Ps. 35 (36).
   R. v. 7: 'How precious, O God, is your love.'

138 Ps. 49 (50) 7–8, 14–23.
   R. v. 23: 'To the upright man I will show how God can save.'

139 Ps. 50 (51).
   R. 12: 'Be my saviour again, renew my joy.'

140 Ps. 72 (73).

R.v. 28: 'My joy lies in being close to God.'

141 Ps. 89 (90).
R. v. 14: 'Let us sing and be happy all our days.'

142 Ps. 94 (95).
R. v. 7: 'If only you would listen to him today.'

143 Ps. 118 (119) 1; 10–13; 15–16.
R. v. 1: 'Happy are those of blameless life, who walk in the Law of the Lord.'

144 Ps. 122 (123).
R. v. 1: 'I lift my eyes to you.'

145 Ps. 129 (130).
R. v. 7: 'With him mercy is to be found, and a generous redemption.'

146 Ps. 138 (139) 1–18; 23–24.
R. v. 23: 'Examine me and know my heart.'

147 Ps. 142 (143) 1–11.
R. v. 10: 'Teach me to obey you, since you are my God.'

New Testament readings

148 Rom. 3: 22–26: 'Justified through the free gift of his grace by being redeemed in Christ Jesus.'

149 Rom. 5: 6–11: 'We are filled with joyful trust in God, through our Lord Jesus Christ, through whom we have already gained our reconciliation.'

150 Rom. 6: 2–13: 'You must consider yourselves to be dead to sin but alive for God in Christ Jesus.'

151 Rom. 6: 16–23: 'The wage paid by sin is death; the present given by God is eternal life in Christ Jesus our Lord.'

152 Rom. 7: 14–25: 'What a wretched man I am! Who will rescue me from this body doomed to death? Thanks be to God through Jesus Christ our Lord.'

153 Rom. 12: 1–2, 9–19: 'Let your behaviour change, model-led by your new mind.'

154 Rom. 13: 8–14: 'Let us give up all the things we prefer to do under cover of the dark; let us arm ourselves and appear in the light.'

155 II Cor. 5: 17–21: 'It was God who reconciled us to himself through Christ.'

156 Gal. 5: 16–24: 'You cannot belong to Christ unless you crucify all self-indulgent passions and desires.'

157 Eph. 2: 1–10: 'But God loved us with so much love that he was generous in his mercy: when we were dead through our sins, he brought us to life with Christ.'

158 Eph. 4: 1–3; 17–32: 'Your mind must be renewed by a spiritual revolution so that you can put on the new self.'

159 Eph. 5: 1–14: 'You were darkness once, but now you are light in the Lord. Be like children of light.'

160 Eph. 6: 10–18: 'Put God's armour on so as to be able to resist the devil's tactics.'

161 Col. 3: 1–10, 12–17: 'Since you have been brought back to true life with Christ, you must look for the things that are in heaven . . . you must kill everything in you that belongs only to earthly life.'

162 Heb. 12: 1–5: 'In the fight against sin, you have not yet had to keep fighting to the point of death.'

163 James 1: 22–27: 'You must do what the word tells you, and not just listen to it.'

164 James 2: 14–26: 'Faith without good deeds is useless.'

165 James 3: 1–12: 'The only man who could reach perfection would be someone who never said anything wrong.'

166 I Peter 1: 13–23: 'The ransom that was paid to free you . . . was not paid in anything corruptible, neither silver nor gold, but in the precious blood of a lamb without spot or stain, namely Christ.'

167 II Peter 1: 3–11: 'You have been called and chosen. Work all the harder to justify it.'

168 I John 1: 5–10; 2: 1–2: 'If we acknowledge our sins, then God who is faithful and just will forgive our sins and purify us from everything that is wrong.'

169 I John 2: 3–11: 'Anyone who hates his brother is still in the dark.'

170 I John 3: 1–24: 'We have passed out of death and into life, and of this we can be sure because we love our brothers.'

171 I John 4: 16–21: 'God is love, and anyone who lives in love lives in God.'

172 Rev. 2: 1–5: 'Repent, and do as you used to at first.'

173 Rev 3: 14–22: 'Since you are neither cold nor hot but lukewarm, I will spit you out of my mouth.'

174 Rev. 20: 11–15: 'The record of what they had done in their lives, by which the dead were judged.'

175 Rev. 21: 1–8: 'It is the rightful inheritance of the one who proves victorious, and I will be his God, and he a son to me.'

176 Matt. 3: 1–12: 'Repent, for the kingdom of heaven is close at hand.'

177 Matt. 4: 12–17: 'Repent, for the kingdom of heaven is close at hand.'

178 Matt. 5: 1–12: 'Seeing the crowds he went up the hill. There he was joined by his disciples . . . This is what he taught them.'

179 Matt. 5: 13–16: 'Your light must shine in the sight of men.'

180 Matt. 5: 17–47: 'Do not imagine that I have come to abolish the Law.'

181 Matt. 9: 1–8: 'Courage, my child, your sins are forgiven.'

182 Matt. 9: 9–13: 'I did not come to call the virtuous, but sinners.'

183 Matt. 18: 15–20: 'If he listens to you, you have won back your brother.'

184 Matt. 18: 21–35: 'That is how my heavenly Father will deal with you unless you each forgive your brother from your heart.'

185 Matt. 25: 31–46: 'In so far as you did this to one of the least of these brothers of mine, you did it to me.'

186 Matt. 26: 69–75: 'He went outside and wept bitterly.'

187 Mark 12: 28–34: 'Which is the first of all the commandments?'

188 Luke 7: 36–50: 'Her sins must have been forgiven her, or she would not have shown such great love.'

189 Luke 13: 1–5: 'Unless you repent you will all perish as they did.'

190 Luke 15: 1–10: 'There is rejoicing among the angels of God over one repentant sinner.'

191 Luke 15: 11–32: 'While he was still a long way off, his father saw him and was moved with pity. He ran to the boy, clasped him in his arms and kissed him tenderly.'

192 Luke 17: 1–4: 'If your brother wrongs you seven times a day and seven times comes back to you and says "I am sorry", you must forgive him.'

193 Luke 18: 9–14: 'God, be merciful to me, a sinner.'

194 Luke 19: 1–10: 'The Son of Man has come to seek out and save what was lost.'

195 Luke 23: 39–43: 'Today you will be with me in paradise.'

196 John 8: 1–11: 'Go away, and don't sin any more.'

197 John 8: 31–36: 'Everyone who commits sin is a slave of sin.'
198 John 15: 1–8: 'Every branch in me that bears no fruit he cuts away, and every branch that does bear fruit he prunes to make it bear even more.'
199 John 15: 9–14: 'You are my friends if you do what I command you.'
200 John 19: 13–37: 'They will look on the one whom they have pierced.'
201 John 20: 19–23: 'Receive the Holy Spirit. For those whose sins you forgive, they are forgiven.'

Preparation for general confession

202 Prayers to God the Father:

1 —My brothers and sisters, God is almighty and merciful. He does not wish for the death of a sinner, but rather that he should turn from his wickedness and live. As we repent for our past sins, let us pray that we may have no cause to weep for sin in the future.

R. Lord, spare your people.

2 —God in his infinite mercy forgives the sins and offences of those who repent. Let us confidently pray to Him in his kindness, that He may grant forgiveness of all their sins to those who confess them with all their heart.

R. We beseech you, hear us.

3 —God gave his Son for our sins and raised him up for our justification. Let us humbly pray to Him, saying:

R. Have mercy on your people, Lord.

4 God our Father looks for the return of his children who have strayed, and embraces them when they come back to him. Let us pray that He may lovingly welcome those who return to His house.

R. We have sinned, Lord, but do not look upon our sins.

or:

Father, we have sinned against you. We are no longer worthy to be called your children.

5 —Let us pray to God who seeks out the lost, brings back the rejected, binds up the broken, and strengthens the weak.

R. Lord, heal our infirmities.

203 Prayers to Christ:

1 —Let us pray to Christ, the victor over sin and death, that we

may receive pardon for our offences against God, and reconciliation with the church that we have wounded through our sins.

R. Lord Jesus, save us.

2 —For the sins of all mankind Christ willingly underwent suffering and death, because he loved us greatly and desired our salvation. Let us approach him with confident prayer and sure hope.

R. Christ, hear us.

3 Let us pray to Christ the good shepherd, who goes out to seek the lost sheep and takes it up in his arms with joy.

R. Come to us Lord, and take us to yourself.

4 My brothers and sisters, let us pray to Christ with humility and trust. He has borne our sins on the cross, and healed us by his wounds. Since we are dead to sin let us devote our lives to all that is good. Let us all say to him:

R. Lord, to whom shall we go? You have the words of eternal life. And we have believed, and we know that you are the Christ, the Son of God.

or:

Have mercy on us and help us.

5 —Let us pray to Christ our Lord who was given up for our sins and rose for our justification. Let us say to him:

R. You are our Saviour.

or:

Christ, Son of the living God, have mercy on us.

Penitential bidding prayers. One of these should always be selected as a petition for true contrition.

204 Prayers to God the Father:

1 —We have sinned and offended against the church by our weakness. May we be truly forgiven for our faults, and restored to full communion with our brothers.

R. We beseech you, hear us.

or:

Have mercy on us, Lord.

or any other response which may be considered suitable.

—Since we trust only in your mercy, may we be admitted to the sacrament of reconciliation. *R.*

—May we strive for the conversion of our brethren with a sincere heart, with charity and prayer. *R.*

—Since we confess our sins today, may we be freed from the slavery of sin and led to the freedom that befits your children. *R.*

—Being reconciled to you, and among ourselves, may we be living witnesses of your love in the world. *R.*

—Through the sacrament of reconciliation, may we receive your peace more abundantly, and seek for its establishment in the world more zealously. *R.*

—Through this sign of your love by which our sins are forgiven, let us learn to love our brethren and forgive them their trespasses. *R.*

—Since we have been clothed in wedding garments through the forgiveness of our sins, grant that we may deserve to approach your holy banquet. *R.*

—With our sins forgiven, lead us by paths of righteousness and love to the possession of everlasting peace. *R.*

—May your light dispel our darkness and guide us in the way of truth. *R.*

—Since we are justly afflicted for our sins, may we be freed from them for the glory of your name. *R.*

—In your love, you have absolved us from the bonds of sin. Keep us from all adversity by your powerful protection. *R.*

—Look upon our weakness, and do not condemn us in your anger for our sinfulness. Purify us in your great mercy, teach us and save us. *R.*

—May your mercy cast out what is old in us, and make us fit to receive the newness of a holy life. *R.*

—May those who have wandered away from you be brought back to the way of justice, love and peace. *R.*

—May your redeeming mercy overcome the evil ways that have harmed us in the past. *R.*

—Put away all our past sins from us, and prepare us for eternal life. *R.*

2 The response may be repeated or varied, as in the Liturgy of the Hours.

—Forgive us for the sins we have committed against the unity of your family,

R. And grant us to be of one heart and one soul.

—We have sinned, Lord, we have sinned,

R. Wipe away our faults by your saving grace.

—Grant to us sinners the grace to implore your forgiveness.

R. and to be reconciled to your church.

—Help us to foster our friendship with you more and more through a sincere conversion,

R. and to make reparation for having offended against your wisdom and goodness.

—Purify and renew your church, O Lord

R. that it may bear witness to you more effectively.

—Touch the hearts of all who have turned away from you through sin and the scandal of others.

R. May they return to you and remain in your love.

—Grant that we may bear in our bodies the death of your son

R. who gave us life through his body.

—O Lord hear the supplications of those who confess their sins

R. and grant us pardon and peace.

—We have sinned greatly, Lord, but we trust in your mercy

R. Bring us back, that we may be truly converted.

—Receive us back with contrite hearts, humbled in spirit,

R. for there is no shame for those who trust in you.

—We have sinned and done evil in turning away from you

R. we have failed in every way, and have not followed your commandments

—Turn to us Lord, have mercy on us and put away our wrong doing.

R. and cast our sins into the depths of the sea.

—Grant us to rejoice, Lord, when we are justified

R. that we may glory in uprightness of heart.

205 Prayers to Christ:

1—Through your death you have reconciled us to the Father and saved us.

R. Lord have mercy, *or* Christ hear us.

(Any other form of response may be used if considered more suitable.)

—You died and rose again. You are seated at the Father's right hand to make intercession for us.

R. Rom. 8: 34.

—You have become our wisdom, our virtue, our holiness and our freedom.

R. I Cor. 1: 30.

—You have washed all men clean, sanctifying and justifying them in the Spirit of our God.

R. I Cor. 6: 11.

You have said that by sinning against our brothers we sin against you.

R. I Cor. 8: 12.

—You became poor for our sake, when you were rich, to make us rich out of your poverty. R. (Cor. 8: 9)

—You sacrificed yourself for our sins to rescue us from the wickedness that surrounds us. R. (Gal. 1: 4)

—You were raised from the dead, to save us from the retribution which is coming. R. (I Th 1: 10)

—You came into the world to save sinners. R. (I Tim. 1: 15)

—You gave yourself as a redemption for all men. R. (I Tim. 2: 6)

—You abolished death and proclaimed life. R. (II Tim. 1: 10)

—You will come to judge the living and the dead. R. (II Tim. 4: 1)

—You sacrificed yourself for us in order to set us free from all wickedness, and to purify a people so that it could be your very own, and would have no ambition except to do good. R. (Tit. 2: 14).

—You became a compassionate and trustworthy high priest of God's religion, able to atone for human sins. R. (Heb. 2: 17)

—For all who obey, you became the source of eternal salvation (Heb. 5: 9)

—Through the Holy Spirit, you offered yourself as the perfect sacrifice to God, purifying our inner self from dead actions. R. (Heb. 9: 14)

—You offered yourself, to take the sins of many on yourself. R. (Heb. 9: 28)

—Innocent though you were, you died once for sins, you died for the guilty. R. (I Peter 3: 18)

—You are the sacrifice that takes our sins away, and not only ours but the whole world's. R. (I John 2: 2)

—You died so that those who believe in you should not perish, but have eternal life. R. (John 3: 16, 35)

—You came into this world to look for what was lost, and to save it. R. (Matt. 18: 11)

—You were sent by the Father, not to judge the world, but so that through you the world might be saved. R. (John 3: 17)

—You have authority on earth to forgive sins. R. (Mark 2: 10)

—You call to yourself all who labour and are overburdened, to give them rest. R. (Matt. 11: 28)

—You gave to your Apostles the keys of the kingdom of heaven, so that they might bind and loose. R. (Matt. 16: 19; 18: 18)

—You summed up the whole law in the love of God and of our neighbour. R. (Matt. 22: 38–40)

—Jesus, you are the life of all men. You came into the world so that all might have life, and have it to the full. R. (John 10: 10)

—Jesus, you are the good Shepherd, who laid down your life for your sheep. R. (John 10: 11)
—Jesus, you are the eternal truth which has made us free (John 8: 32)
—Jesus, you are the only way, and no one can come to the Father except through you. R. (John 14: 6)
—Jesus, you are the resurrection and the life. Those who believe in you, even though they die, will live. R. (John 11: 25)
—Jesus, you are the true vine. Every one of your branches that bears fruit is pruned by the Father so that it may bear even more. R. (John 15: 1–2)

2 The response may be repeated or varied, as in the Liturgy of the Hours.

—Healer of bodies and souls, cure us of the wounds in our hearts
R. and may your holiness be a protection to us.
—Grant that we may put off the old man with all his works
R. and put on the new man, which is yourself.
—May we come closer to you, our Redeemer, through penance
R. that we may attain to the glory of the resurrection.
—May your mother, the refuge of sinners, intercede for us
R. that you in your goodness may forgive us our sins.
—You forgave the sins of the penitent woman
R. in your mercy do not turn away from us.
—You carried on your shoulders the sheep that had gone astray,
R. receive us into your kingdom.
—You died for us, and rose again
R. grant us a share in your death and resurrection.

206 Acts of praise
Ps. 31 (32), 1–7; 10–11.
R. Rejoice in the Lord, and exult, you virtuous.
Ps. 97 (98), 1–9.
R. The Lord has remembered his mercy.
Ps. 99 (100), 2–5.
—The Lord is good, his love is everlasting.
Ps. 118 (119), 1; 10–13; 15–16; 18; 33; 105; 169; 170; 174–175.
R. Blessed are you Lord, teach me your statues.
Ps. 102 (103), 1–4; 8–18.
R. The Lord's love for those who fear him, lasts from all eternity, and for ever.

Ps. 144 (145), 1–21.
R. I bless your name for ever and ever, Lord, blessing you day after day.
Ps. 145 (146), 2–10.
R. I will praise God all my life.
Is. 12: 1b–6.
R. Praise the Lord, and call on his holy name.
Is. 61: 10–11.
—My soul exults in my God.
Jer. 31: 10–14.
—The Lord has redeemed his people.
Dan. 3: 52–57.
R. Bless the Lord, all you works of the Lord, praise and extoll him for ever.
Luke 1: 46–55.
R. The Lord has remembered his mercy.
Eph. 1: 3–10.
—Blessed be the Lord, who chose us in Christ.
Rev. 15: 3–4.
R. Your works are great and wonderful, O Lord.

Concluding prayer

207 It is right and fitting that we should give you thanks, always and everywhere, almighty and eternal God. You show your mercy by chastening us and forgiving us. You have established a law for us, by which we are held in check, so that we may not perish for ever. You spare us, and give us time to correct our faults. Through Christ our Lord. Amen.

208 Lord God, creator and ruler of the light, you so loved the world that you gave your only begotten son for our salvation. By his cross we are redeemed, and through his death we have received life. His passion has saved us, and his resurrection has glorified us. Through him we pray you to be with this family in every way. Let their be faith in our hearts, justice and kindness in our works, and truth on our lips. Let there be discipline in our ways, reverence and devotion in our mind and heart, that we may attain worthily to the gift of eternal life. Through Christ our Lord.

209 Lord Jesus Christ, you are generous in your forgiveness. You took on a human nature so that we might have the example of your humility, and be constant in all sufferings. Grant that we may hold fast to the good things we have received from you. Whenever we fall into sin, may we be lifted up again by penance. Who live and reign for ever and ever. Amen.

210 O God, you give us sinners the grace to become virtuous, and turn our wretchedness into blessedness. Support us in our actions and foster your gifts in us, so that we who have been justified by faith may not lack the fortitude to persevere, through Christ our Lord. Amen.

211 God our Father, you have taken away our sins and given us your peace. Help us to forgive when we offend one another, that we may bring about peace in the world. Through Christ our Lord. Amen.

The blessing

212 May the blessing of Almighty God, the Father and the Son and the Holy Spirit, come down upon you and remain with you always. Amen.

213 May we be blessed by the Father who has given us eternal life. Amen.

May the Son who died and rose again for us grant us salvation. Amen.

May the Spirit poured out in our hearts sanctify us, and lead us in the right path. Amen.

214 May the Father bless us, who has called us to be his adopted sons. Amen.

May the Son come to our help, who has made us his brothers. Amen.

May the Spirit be with us, who has made us his temple. Amen.

Appendix I

Absolution from Censures

1 In the case of a reserved sin or censure, the usual absolution is given. It is sufficient that the confessor should intend to absolve the penitent, if properly disposed, of his reserved sins, provided (and unless anything else is stated or done in the law) the penitent is prepared to have recourse to the competent authority. The confessor, before absolving the penitent's sins, can absolve the censure with the form given below, outside the sacrament of penance.

2 When a priest is absolving a penitent from censure outside the sacrament of penance, the following form is used:
—With the authority granted to me I absolve you from the bond of excommunication (or suspension or interdict). In the name of the Father, and of the Son ✠ and of the Holy Spirit.
The penitent answers: Amen.

Dispensation from Irregularity

3 If a penitent is bound by some irregularity, a priest can dispense from the irregularity in confession, after absolution has been given, or outside the sacramental of penance, saying:
—With the power granted to me I dispense you from the irregularity you have incurred. In the name of the Father and of the Son ✠ and of the Holy Spirit.
The penitent answers: Amen.

Appendix II

Specimen Penitential Services

The following part has been drawn up by the Sacred Congregation for Divine Worship for the use of those who are required to arrange or produce penitential services.

Penitential Services

Foreword

1 Penitential services are useful both in the life of the individual and of the community, for encouraging a spirit of repentance, and for preparing people for a more fruitful reception of the sacrament of penance. Care should be taken that the faithful do not get the impression that penitential services are the same thing as the sacrament of penance.

2 Penitential services, especially those designed for specific groups, should take into account the mentality and speech of the congregation. Liturgical commissions, and all those who draw up penitential services, should select the texts most suited to the needs of each congregation.

3 To this end, a variety of penitential services is offered. These are to be taken as specimens, to be adapted in their turn to the specific needs of local communities.

4 When the sacrament of penance is administered in these services, the rite of reconciliation of a group of penitents, with individual confession and absolution is used, see **48** ff. But in special cases envisaged in the law, the reconciliation of a group of penitents with general confession and absolution is used, see **60** ff.

I Penitential Services in Lent

5 Lent is the principal time of penance for individual Christians and for the whole Church. It is fitting therefore that there should be penitential services during this season, so that the Christian

community may be more fully prepared for sharing in the paschal mystery.

6 The penitential character of the service of the word in Lenten masses should be borne in mind. Texts from the Missal and the Lectionary may be used in Lenten penitential services.

7 The following two services have been devised for Lent. The first deals with penance as a help in strengthening or restoring the grace of baptism. The second shows how penance is a preparation for participating more fully in the paschal mystery of Christ and the Church.

I Penance strengthens and restores the grace of baptism

8 (a) A hymn is sung and the minister greets the people. The faithful are told about the significance of this service, which prepares the Christian community to re-affirm the grace of baptism at the Easter vigil, and to begin a new life with Christ through the forgiveness of sins.

9 (b) **Prayer:**

—My brothers and sisters, our sins have made us forgetful of the grace we received in baptism. Let us pray that we may be restored to that grace by doing penance.

Let us kneel and pray (*or:* Bow down your heads before God).

(All pray for a while in silence.)

—Rise up.

—Lord, in your unchanging love you have washed our sins away and redeemed us by your passion. Protect us always in that same love, that we may rejoice in your resurrection. You who live and reign for ever and ever.

R. Amen.

10 (c) **Readings**

Just as the Israelites, having crossed the Red Sea, became forgetful of the wonderful intervention of God on their behalf, so do God's people, having received the grace of baptism, often return to their former sins.

I Cor. 10: 1–13: 'I want to remind you, brothers. . . .'

Ps. 105, 6–10; 13–14; 19–22; *R.* (6)

—The son who abandoned his father and his home is lovingly welcomed back again by his father. The shepherd goes to great trouble to find the sheep that has wandered away from the flock. God seeks us when we have sinned after receiving the grace of baptism, and when we return to him he takes us back to himself with love, and the whole church rejoices.

Luke 15, 4–7: He spoke this parable to them: 'What man among you with a hundred sheep. . . .'

or Luke 15, 11–32: He also said: 'A man had two sons. . . .'

11 (d) **Homily, on any of the following:**

—the need to live up to the grace of baptism by being faithful to Christ's gospel (see I Cor. 10: 1–13)

—the gravity of sin committed after baptism (see Heb. 6: 4–8)

—the infinite mercy of our God and Father who welcomes us back to himself, over and over again, after we have sinned and turned back to him (see Luke 15)

—the Easter festival is a time of rejoicing for the church because the catechumens are baptised and penitents are reconciled.

12 (e) **Examination of conscience**

This will be found in Appendix III, p. 164. There should always be a sufficient time of silence for all the faithful to examine their conscience in their own way. There should be special reference here to the baptismal promises, to be renewed at the Easter vigil.

13 (f) **Act of repentance (by the deacon or another minister)**

—My brothers and sisters, this is the acceptable time, the day of divine mercy and the salvation of men. Death is overcome and eternal life begins. In the Lord's vineyard new vines are to be planted, and the old vines will be pruned so that they may bear more fruit.

—Each one of us confesses that he is a sinner. Each of us is encouraged by the example of his brothers, and moved by their prayers, readily admits: 'I acknowledge my sins, they are always before me. Turn away your face from them, Lord, and wash them all away. Give me back the joy of your salvation, and strengthen your spirit within me.'

—Since we come as suppliants with sorrowful hearts to beg God's mercy, may he come to our aid. We have displeased him in the past by our misdeeds. Let us rejoice now with the risen Lord who has given us life, that we may please God in the land of the living.

The priest sprinkles the congregation with holy water as they sing:

Sprinkle me with hyssop and I shall be clean,
wash me and I shall be made whiter than snow.

The priest then prays:
—O God, you are the loving creator of the human race. You have
made us new in your great mercy. The devil's envy deprived us
of eternal life, but you have redeemed us by the blood of
your Son. To us whose death you do not desire give your Holy
Spirit. You have no wish that we should perish for our sins. You do
not abandon us when we turn away from you. Take us to yourself now that we have been chastened by penitence. Accept our
humble and trusting confession. Heal our wounds. Hold out your
hand to save the fallen, so that no part of your church may suffer
loss. May the evil one not exult in the destruction of your flock
and its condemnation. May those who have been reborn in the
waters of salvation not undergo a second death. We pour out our
prayers and our tears to you, Lord. Spare us as we confess our sins,
that we may be brought back from the error of our ways to the
path of holiness. Let your flock suffer no further wounds. Let it
remain whole forever through your grace and your mercy.
Through our Lord Jesus Christ your Son who lives and reigns
with you in the unity of the Holy Spirit, God, world without end.
R. Amen.
A hymn is then sung, and the congregation dismissed.

II Penance as a preparation for a fuller share in the paschal mystery of Christ for the salvation of the world

14 (a) A hymn is sung and the minister greets the people. There
is a brief introduction in which the people are reminded of the
social aspect both of sin and penance. They are a community,
and it is for the sanctification of the whole community that each
one is called upon to change his way of life.

15 (b) **Prayer:**
—My brothers and sisters, Christ was crucified for our sins. Let
us be united to him through penance, so that we may share with
all men in his resurrection.
—Let us kneel and pray (or: Bow down your heads before God).
   (All pray in silence for a while.)
—Rise up.
—Lord, our God and Father, you gave us life through the passion

145

of your Son. Grant that we, being united to his death by penance, may share with all men in his resurrection. Through Christ our Lord. Amen.

or :

—Grant, almighty and merciful Father, that, moved and strengthened by your Spirit, we may always bear in our bodies the death of Christ, so that we may show forth his life. Through Christ our Lord. Amen.

16 (c) Readings

—The Lord's servant bears the sins of the people like a gentle lamb, and by his wounds they are healed. Christ's disciples can make expiation for the sins of the whole world by doing penance. Is. 53: 1–7; 10–12: 'Who could believe what we have heard...?'

—God hears the prayers of Christ who died on the cross for our sins. His death has become the life of the whole world. Through penance we die to our sins, and renew the life of the church and of the world.

Ps 21 (22), 2–3; 7–9; 18–28.

—If we bear patiently with the sufferings that are natural to us, or are inflicted on us by our fellow men, we are imitating Christ. Our love can overcome hatred in the world. We can overcome evil with good. We are sharing in Christ's passion and so bringing life into the world.

I Peter 2: 20–25: 'The merit, in the sight of God, is in bearing it patiently....'

Verse before the gospel:

Glory to you Lord, for you were given up for our sins, and you rose again to make us holy. Glory to you Lord.

(or a suitable hymn)

—Jesus exhorts his disciples to follow his example. They are to drink of his cup. Every man is to be the servant of his brother, and ready to lay down his life for him.

Mark 10: 32–45. Shorter version, Mark 10: 32–34; 42–45: 'They were on the road, going up to Jerusalem....'

17 (d) The homily, on any of the following:

—By sin we offend not only against God but also against the body of Christ, the church, of which we became members through our baptism.

—Sin is a lack of love for Christ, who loved us to the uttermost.

—Whether we do good or evil, we do it together as a society.

—Christ suffers for us. He bears our sins and we are healed through his wounds (see Is. 53; I Peter 2: 24).
—the social aspect of penance in the church. The conversion of each member has its effect on the whole community.
—Easter is a festival of the Christian community, which renews itself through the conversion or penance of each member, and is thus able to witness more clearly to salvation in the world.

18 (e) **Examination of conscience**
The formula found in Appendix III, p. 164, may be used. There should always be a sufficient time of silence for all the faithful to examine their conscience in their own way.

19 (f) **Act of repentance**
All say together:
 I confess to almighty God and to you, my brothers and sisters, that I have sinned through my own fault (they strike their breast) in my thoughts and in my words, in what I have done and in what I have failed to do; and I ask blessed Mary, ever virgin, all the angels and saints, and you my brothers and sisters, to pray for me to the Lord our God.
 The minister then suggests various acts of loving service towards the brethren, as for instance giving alms to the poor, visiting the sick, or making reparation for some injustice committed in the community, etc. So that they may celebrate the paschal mystery with joy.
 The Lord's prayer is then said or sung, and the minister concludes it thus:
—Deliver us, Father, from all evil, and through the blessed passion of your Son, to which our repentance unites us, grant us a share in his joyful resurrection. Through Christ our Lord.
R. Amen.

 This may be followed by adoration of the cross, or the stations of the cross, and after a final hymn, the priest dismisses the congregation with his blessing.

II   *A Penitential Service for Advent*

20 (a) A hymn is sung and the celebrant greets the people with a brief summary of the significance of the ceremony:
—My brothers and sisters, Advent is a time of preparation. We

are looking forward to celebrating the mystery of Our Lord's Incarnation, from which our salvation drew its origin. At the same time we are also awaiting Our Lord's second coming, which will bring the history of our salvation to its fulfilment. As we read in the gospel, 'Happy those servants whom the master finds awake when he comes' (Luke 12, 37). This reminds us that we must be vigilant, since Our Lord will come to each one of us at the hour of our death. May this penitential service purify us and make us more ready to welcome our Lord at his coming, which we shall celebrate in the liturgy.

or:

My brothers and sisters, the time has come: we must wake up now. Our salvation is even nearer than it was when we began to believe. The night is almost over, it will be daylight soon—let us give up all the things we prefer to do under cover of the dark. Let us arm ourselves and appear in the light (Rom. 13: 11-12).

21 (b) **Prayer:**

—Let us pray, brethren, that our Lord's coming, which we shall soon be celebrating with all solemnity in the liturgy of Christmas may find us ready and alert.

(All pray for a while in silence.)

—Let us pray to God, the creator of heaven, that he may pardon the offences we have committed, as we await the coming of our Redeemer. Through Christ our Lord.

R. Amen.

or:

—Son of God, creator and sinless saviour of the human race, come, we pray you, from the Immaculate Virgin's womb and redeem the world. By the grace of your coming to us and sharing our nature in all things but sin, may we be delivered from all evil. You who live and reign for ever and ever.

R. Amen.

22 (c) **Readings**

—The Lord's coming brings judgment. We are choosing our reward or our punishment in this present life through the things we do. When the Lord appears, our choice will become apparent. Repentance is a moment of choosing and deciding.

Mal. 3: 1-7: 'Look, I am going to send my messenger. . . .'

—God sent his son into the world, not to condemn it, but to save it. The Lord's coming, which we now celebrate as a mystery, is the coming of salvation. We are celebrating this service of repentance because we look forward to the Lord's nativity, to our salvation, and to his final coming.

Ps. 84 (85), R. v. 8.

—When our Lord Jesus comes, he will take us into a new life, a new world. The church is the living of the holy city which has yet to be fully revealed. Only sin excludes us from it.

Rev. 21: 1–12: 'Then I saw a new heaven and a new earth. . . .'

Verse before the gospel:

—The Lord says, 'I am coming soon, bringing the reward to be given to every man according to what he deserves.' Come, Lord Jesus.

or:

—The Spirit and the Bride says, 'Come'. Let everyone who listens answer, 'Come'. Come, Lord Jesus (Rev. 22: 12; 17: 20).

(A hymn may be sung instead.)

—As in the days of John the Baptist, so for us today, the Lord's coming is a time of conversion and repentance, so that we may receive salvation from him when he comes.

John 3: 1–12: 'In due course, John the Baptist appeared. . . .'

or: Luke 3: 3–17: 'He went through the whole Jordan district. . . .'

23 (d) Homily. Examination of conscience

A formula will be found in Appendix III, p. 164. There should be a sufficient time of silence for all to examine their consciences in their own way.

24 (e) Act of repentance

I confess, etc., as in the other penitential services. Then follows the Lord's prayer, which the celebrant concludes thus:

—O God, you created light at the beginning of the world, and dispelled darkness. You decreed from all eternity that your Son, in whom the light came to be, should come now to free us from original sin. Grant that we may go out to meet him, prepared for his coming by repentance and good works. Through Christ our Lord. R. Amen.

or:

—Almighty and eternal God, you have reconciled the world to yourself by the Incarnation of your only Son. Grant that our hearts may be made free from sin, so that we may always celebrate his birth with joy. Through Christ our Lord. R. Amen.

(This is followed by the hymn and final blessing.)

III *Penitential Services for any time of the year*

A. Theme: Sin and Conversion

25 (a) After a suitable hymn or psalm (e.g. Ps. 138 (139), vv. 1–12; 16; 23–24) and greeting, the minister briefly summarises the readings that will be heard. He then invites the congregation to pray for a while in silence, and concludes:

Lord Jesus, when Peter denied you three times, you turned and looked at him, so that he would weep for his sin and turn back to you with all his heart. Look now on us, and move our hearts so that we may return to you, and follow you faithfully for the rest of our lives, you who live and reign for ever and ever. Amen.

26 (b) Readings

Luke 22: 21–34. 'I tell you, Peter, by the time the cock crows today you will have denied three times that you know me.'
A brief silence follows.
Luke 22: 54–62. 'Peter went outside and wept bitterly.' Ps. 30 (31), vv. 10; 15–17; 20 or Ps. 50 (51), or a hymn.
John 21: 15–19. 'Simon son of John, do you love me?'

27 (c) Homily, on any of the following subjects:

—that we must put our trust in the grace of God, and not in our own strength;
—that we must be faithful to our baptismal promises if we are to be truly the Lord's disciples.
—that our weakness often causes us to sin and so fail to be witnesses to the gospel.
—that the Lord is merciful, and that if we turn to him with our whole heart, after we have sinned, he will take us back into his friendship.

28 (d) Examination of conscience

Examples will be found in Appendix III, p. 164. Sufficient time must be given so that everyone may be able to examine his conscience thoroughly in his own way.

29 (e) Act of repentance

The minister now invites the congregation to pray, using these or similar words:
—God commends his love to us in that he loved us first. While we were still in our sins, he had mercy on us. So let us turn to him

now with our whole heart, and let us, like Peter, tell him humbly that we love him:

R. Lord, you know all things; you know that I love you.

(There should be a short pause between the invocations, which may be read by different members of the congregation, while the whole assembly joins in the response.)

—We, like Peter, have trusted in ourselves rather than in your grace. Turn to us Lord, and have mercy on us.

R. Lord, you know all things; you know that I love you.

—We have acted without humility and without prudence, and so have fallen into sin. Turn to us Lord, and have mercy on us. R.

—We have been proud, and thought ourselves better than others. Turn to us, Lord, and have mercy on us. R.

—There have been times when we were glad, rather than sorry, to see our brothers fallen from grace. Turn to us Lord, and have mercy on us. R.

—We have shown contempt, instead of going to the help of those in trouble. Turn to us Lord, and have mercy on us. R.

—We have failed to give witness to truth and justice, through fear of the consequences. Turn to us Lord, and have mercy on us. R.

—We have often been unfaithful to those baptismal promises by which we became your disciples. Turn to us, Lord, and have mercy on us. R.

—Let us turn to our Father in prayer, and beg him to forgive us our sins, in the words that Christ gave us:

Our Father....

30 An appropriate hymn or psalm is now sung, and the minister dismisses the congregation with the following prayer:

Lord Jesus, our Saviour, you called Peter to be an apostle, and he sinned. When he repented, you took him back into your friendship, and confirmed him in his apostolate and made him chief of the apostles. Look upon us now, and bring us back to you, so that we may follow Peter's example, following you henceforward with a greater love, who live and reign for ever and ever. Amen.

B Theme: The Prodigal Son

31 (a) After a suitable hymn or psalm has been sung, the minister explains the theme to the congregation. He invites them to pray for a while in silence, and concludes:

—Lord God Almighty, you are the Father of all. You created men so that they might live for ever with you in your house, to the praise of your glory. Make us attentive to your call so that having departed from you through our sins, we may return to you with all our heart. Let us come to know that you are our Father, full of mercy to those who call upon you. You punish us, but only so that we may turn away from sin, and you forgive us all the wrong we have done. Give us the joy of your salvation, so that when we return to you, we may join in the feast in your house, now and forever. Amen.

32 (b) Readings
Eph. 1 : 3–7. 'He determined that we should become his adopted sons.'
Ps. 26 (27), 1; 4; 7–10; 13–14.
Luke 15 : 11–32. 'His father saw him and was moved with pity.'

33 (c) Homily, on any of the following subjects:
—sin is a turning away from the love that we owe to God our Father.
—God's infinite mercy towards his sinful children.
—the nature of true conversion.
—we must always forgive our fellow men.
—the Eucharistic banquet as the fulness of reconciliation between God and his church.

34 (d) Examination of conscience
Examples will be found in Appendix III, p. 164. Sufficient time must be given so that everyone may be able to examine his conscience thoroughly in his own way.

35 (e) Act of repentance
The minister now invites the congregation to pray:
 Our God is a God of mercy, slow to anger and very patient. He takes us back, as the father took back his son whom he saw returning while he was still a long way off. With confidence let us say to him:
R. We are not worthy to be called your sons.
—We have used your gifts badly, and sinned against you.
R. We are not worthy to be called your sons.
—We forgot your love when we sinned against you. R.

—We have thought of our own pleasure rather than of our good, and the good of our fellow men, when we sinned against you. *R.*
—We have given little thought to the needs of others when we sinned against you. *R.*
—We were slow to forgive our brothers and so we sinned against you. *R.*
—We have sinned against the mercy that you have so often shown us, when we sinned against you. *R.*
(Further invocations may be added. There should be a short pause between the invocations, which may be read by different members of the congregation.)
—Let us now call upon our Father, using the words that Jesus taught us, that he may forgive us our Sins. Our Father. . . .

36 (f) An appropriate hymn or psalm is now sung, and the minister dismisses the congregation with the following prayer:

God, our Father, you determined that we should become your adopted children, so that we might be holy in your sight, and always happy in your house. Take us to yourself, keep us in your love, that we may live in your holy church in love and happiness. Through Christ our Lord. Amen.

C. Theme: The Beatitudes

37 (a) After a suitable hymn or psalm has been sung, the minister greets the congregation and briefly summarises the readings that will be heard. He then invites the congregation to pray for a while in silence, and concludes:

O Lord, open our hearts today to hear your voice. May we follow your Son's gospel, and through his death and resurrection may we walk in newness of life. Through Christ our Lord. Amen.

38 (b) **Readings**
I John 1: 5–9. 'If we say we have no sin in us, we are deceiving ourselves.'
Ps. 145 (146), 5–10.
Matt. 5: 1–10. 'Blessed are the poor in spirit, for theirs is the kingdom of heaven.'

39 (c) **Homily, on any of the following subjects:**
—When we sin, we are forgetting Christ's commandments and offending against the beatitudes.
—our faith must be strong in the words of Jesus.

—we must follow Christ faithfully, in our lives as individuals, as members of the Christian community, and in the whole human family.

—a homily on any particular beatitude.

40 (d) Examination of conscience

Examples will be found in Appendix III, p. 164. Sufficient time must be given so that everyone may be able to examine his conscience thoroughly in his own way.

41 (e) Act of repentance

The minister now invites the congregation to pray, using these or similar words:

My brothers and sisters, Jesus Christ has left us his example to follow. Let us turn to him in prayer, humbly and trustfully, asking him to purify our hearts, and give us the grace to live according to his gospel.

—Lord Jesus Christ, you said: 'Blessed are the poor in spirit for theirs is the kingdom of heaven.' But we have been too much concerned with wealth, and we have gone about acquiring it unjustly. Lamb of God, who takes away the sins of the world,
R. have mercy on us.

—Lord Jesus Christ, you said 'Blessed are the meek, for they shall inherit the earth.' But we treat each other with violence, and the world is full of discord and war. Lamb of God, who takes away the sins of the world,
R. have mercy on us.

—Lord Jesus Christ, you said: 'Blessed are those who weep, for they shall be consoled.' But we have borne our own sufferings with impatience, and have cared little about the sufferings of others. Lamb of God, who takes away the sins of the world,
R. have mercy on us.

—Lord Jesus Christ, you said: 'Blessed are those who hunger and thirst after justice, for they shall be satisfied.' But we have not thirsted after you, who are the source of all holiness, and we have been indifferent in seeking after justice, whether for individuals or for the public good. Lamb of God, who takes away the sins of the world,
R. have mercy on us.

—Lord Jesus Christ, you said: 'Blessed are the merciful, for they shall obtain mercy.' But we judge our brothers severely, and refuse to forgive them. Lamb of God, who takes away the sins of the world,

R. have mercy on us.

—Lord Jesus Christ, you said: 'Blessed are the pure in heart, for they shall see God.' But we are enslaved by the desires of our senses, and dare not lift up our eyes to you. Lamb of God, who takes away the sins of the world,

R. have mercy on us.

—Lord Jesus Christ, you said: 'Blessed are the peacemakers, for they shall be called the sons of God.' But we are unable to make peace, whether in our families, in society, or in the world. Lamb of God, who takes away the sins of the world,

R. have mercy on us.

—Lord Jesus Christ, you said: 'Blessed are those who suffer persecution for the sake of justice, for theirs is the kingdom of heaven.' But far from suffering for the sake of justice, we behave unjustly, for we discriminate against our fellow men, we oppress and persecute them. Lamb of God, who takes away the sins of the world,

R. have mercy on us.

—Let us now call upon the Lord, that he may deliver us from evil and make us worthy of his kingdom. Our Father. . . .

42 (f) **After a suitable hymn or psalm, the minister concludes with the following prayer:**

—Lord Jesus Christ, you are meek and humble of heart, you are peaceful and merciful. You were poor, and you were put to death for the sake of justice. Through the cross you came into your glory, to show us the way of salvation. Grant us to live up to the gospel joyfully, following your example, so that we may inherit your kingdom and share it with you, who live and reign for ever and ever. Amen.

IV *A Penitential Service for children*

43 This scheme is designed for young children, even those who have not made their first confession.

Theme: Finding the lost sheep

44 The children should be properly prepared for the service in

advance, so as to have a clear idea of what they are doing, and what the service is about. They should be very familiar with the hymns they are going to sing and the responses they are going to make, and they should have at least a rudimentary knowledge of the scripture texts that will be read, of the actions they are going to perfom and their order.

45 (a) **The greeting**
The children are assembled in church or in some suitable place, and the celebrant greets them in friendly fashion, and briefly summarises what is about to take place. A hymn is then sung.

46 (b) **Reading**
The celebrant makes a brief introduction to the reading, e.g.

When we were baptised we all became God's children, and because He is our Father, He loves us and He wants us to love Him very much. He wants us to be good to each other, so that we can all be happy.

Now people don't always do what God asks them to do. They say 'I'll do what I want to do. I won't do what I'm told!' They don't obey God. They won't listen to what he says. And that's what we do very often.

This is what we call sin. It means that we are turning away from God, and if it's something really bad we are doing, then we cut ourselves off from God altogether.

So what does God do when someone turns away from him? When we are going the wrong way and getting lost, what does he do? Does he get angry and turn away from us?

Listen to what he does:

47 **Only one scripture text is read**
Luke 15: 1–7. 'The tax collectors and the sinners, meanwhile, were all seeking his company....'

48 (c) **Homily**
This should be short. It should concentrate on God's love for us, and be a starting point for the examination of conscience.

49 (d) **Examination of conscience**
The celebrant helps with suggestions (cf. Appendix III, p. 164) and a period of silence is observed.

50 (e) Act of repentance

This may be read by the celebrant, or by one or more of the children. Before the response, which all recite or sing together, there should be a brief pause.

God, our Father,

—we have often not behaved as your children should.

R. You love us, and you find us when we are lost.

—We have been troublesome to our parents and our teachers.

R. You love us, and you find us when we are lost.

—We have been fighting, and speaking unkindly to one another.

R. You love us, and you find us when we are lost.

—We have been lazy at home and in school. We have not wanted to help other people.

R. You love us, and you find us when we are lost.

—We have been boastful and we have told lies.

R. You love us, and you find us when we are lost.

—We have not bothered to do good actions when we could.

R. You love us, and you find us when we are lost.

Let us go to our Father, with Jesus our brother, and ask him to forgive us our sins. Our Father....

51 (f) Act of contrition and purpose of amendment

This may be conveyed by some sign, e.g. each child could carry a candle to an altar or shrine (with the minister helping if necessary) and light it here, saying:

Father, I am sorry for all the wrong I have done. I am sorry for not doing the things I should have done. I shall try to do better especially in (some specific purpose of amendment) . . . and to do all I can so as to walk in your light.

Each child could have this prayer written out, with its own purpose of amendment, and could put it on the altar or shrine along with the candle. The candle can be omitted if necessary. If there is a large number of children, they could all say the prayer together, with a general purpose of amendment.

52 (g) The celebrant prays:

God our Father, you always come to find us when we lose our way, and you are always ready to forgive all the wrong we have done. Have mercy on us, forgive us our sins, and lead us to eternal life. R. Amen.

53 A hymn of thanksgiving follows, and the children are dismissed by the celebrant.

54 This should be prepared by the young people themselves if possible. Together with the celebrant they should choose and compose the texts and hymns and themselves read the lessons and sing the hymns.

Theme: Christian vocation and renewal of life

55 (a) We have come together to repent of our sins and to renew our lives. As we do this, we are looking to the future rather than the past, and we are doing something that is more joyful than painful. Through repentance, God is opening up a new road to us, leading us on to the full freedom of the children of God. Christ calls us to turn to him. He shows us the way to his kingdom. We are to be like the man in the parable, who found a pearl of great price, and sold all he had to buy it. As we follow Christ's teaching, we leave behind us our old way of life, so as to possess something far more valuable.

(The hymn or psalm should be about following God's call, e.g. Ps. 39 (40), 1–9 ,with the response: 'Here I am, I am coming to obey your will.')

56 (b) **Prayer:**
O God, you call us out of darkness into your light, from falsehood to truth, and from death to life. You pour your Holy Spirit into our hearts, opening our ears and giving us strength to follow where you call us, and to lead a truly Christian life. Through Christ our Lord. *R*. Amen.

57 (c) **Readings**
Rom. 7: 18–25: 'I know of nothing good living in me. . . .'
or Rom. 8: 19–23: 'The whole creation is eagerly waiting. . . .'
  (Hymn or pause for silence.)
Matt. 13: 44–46: 'The kingdom of heaven is like treasure hidden in a field. . . .'

58 (d) **Homily, on any of the following:**
—The law of sin within us, which fights against God.
—if we wish to enter the kingdom of heaven, we must give up sinful habits.

59 (e) Examination of conscience

An example will be found in Appendix II, p. 164. There should be a sufficient time of silence for all to examine their consciences in their own way.

60 (f) Act of repentance

Christ our Lord called sinners into his kingdom. Let each one of us now make a true act of contrition, and a practical and concrete resolution.

(After a brief pause, all say together.)

I confess to almighty God, and to you, my brothers and sisters, that I have sinned through my own fault (they strike their breast) in my thoughts and in my words, in what I have done and in what I have failed to do; and I ask blessed Mary, ever virgin, all the angels and saints, and you, my brothers and sisters, to pray for me to the Lord our God.

Minister:

Lord, you know all things. You know that we sincerely wish to serve you and our fellow men. Look upon us and hear our prayers.

Reader:

—Give us the grace of true repentance.

R. We beseech you, hear us.

—Rouse up in us a spirit of penance, and strengthen us in our purpose of amendment.

R. We beseech you, hear us.

—Forgive us our sins and have pity on our weakness.

R. We beseech you, hear us.

—Fill our hearts with the spirit of trust and generosity.

R. We beseech you, hear us.

—Make us true disciples of your son, and living members of his church.

R. We beseech you, hear us.

Minister:

O God, you do not wish for the death of the sinner, but rather that he should turn from his wickedness and live. Graciously hear us as we acknowledge our sins, and pour out your mercy on us as we pray, in our Lord's own words: Our Father. . . .

61 (The service concludes with a hymn.)

62 This service can take place in a chapel or in any room where the sick are gathered together. The length of the service, and the texts used, should be adapted to the needs of the patients. If it is not possible for one of the patients to act as reader, someone else should be invited to do so.

Theme: Sickness is to be considered as an occasion of grace

63 (a) **The Greeting**

Jesus preached penance as part of the good news of the gospel. He tells us about the love and mercy of God, which calls us again and again to turn to him, and live our lives for him. Repentance is a gift of God, which we for our part must receive with gratitude. This should be our intention now, as we open our conscience to him, simply and humbly asking him to reconcile us to himself, while we ask forgiveness of each other.

A penitential type of hymn is now sung, either by the patients or by others.

64 (b) **Prayer:**

O God, source of all goodness and mercy, give to your children, gathered together in your name, a spirit of repentance and trust. Begging forgiveness of you and of our fellow men, may we sincerely confess our sins. Grant us to be more fully united to you, and to our brethren, so that we may serve you more worthily. Through Christ our Lord. Amen.

65 (c) **Readings**

An introduction of this type may be used—

Because we are ungrateful and neglectful, we tend to take our health, along with many other good things, for granted. But when we are ill, we realise that health is a great gift. When it is taken away from us, we quickly lose heart. But God allows sickness to prove our faith. Our suffering, when it is a sharing in Christ's passion, can be of great value for ourselves and for the church. The time we spend in being ill is not pointless or wasted. If we can accept it as God wishes us to accept it, it can become a time of special grace. This penitential service aims to help us towards the right dispositions of acceptance. So let us listen now to the word of God, and examine our consciences, and turn to God in prayer.

66 James 5: 13-16: 'If any one of you is in trouble. . . .'

Between the readings a psalm can be read or sung, e.g. Ps. 129 (130) or Ps. 50 (51).

Mark 2: 1-12: 'When he returned to Capernaum. . . .'

67 (d) The Homily
This should treat of sickness, not so much in its physical aspect, but in terms of our spiritual failings. It should emphasise the power of Jesus and the church to forgive sins, and the power of suffering offered up for the benefit of others.

68 (e) Examination of conscience
The following may be added to the texts given in Appendix III, p. 164. Sufficient time must be given so that everyone may be able to examine his conscience thoroughly in his own way.

—Do I trust in God's providence and goodness when I am feeling ill?

—Do I give way to feelings of depression and despair?

—Do I spend my free time thinking about how I should live my life so as to please God, and in communing with him?

—Do I accept sickness and pain as an opportunity for sharing in the sufferings of Christ which redeemed us?

—Do I really believe that I am doing something for the good of the church by accepting suffering with patience?

—Do I think about the needs of my fellow-sufferers, and sympathise with them?

—Am I sufficiently grateful to those who look after me and come to visit me?

—Do I try to give good example as a Christian should?

—Am I sorry for my past sins, and do I offer up my illness and weakness so as to make reparation for them?

69 (f) Penitential rite
After a period of silence, all say together:

I confess to almighty God, and to you my brothers and sisters, that I have sinned through my own fault

(They strike their breast.)

in my thoughts and in my words, in what I have done and in what I have failed to do; and I ask blessed Mary, ever virgin, all the

angels and saints, and you my brothers and sisters, to pray for me
to the Lord our God.

Reader:
—Lord God, we bear the name of your Son and we call you our
Father. We are sorry that we have offended you and injured
our fellow men.
R. Make us truly sorry, and increase our love for you and for our
brothers.
—Lord Jesus Christ, you redeemed us by your passion and cross,
and gave us an example of patience and love. We are sorry that we
have offended you, and neglected to serve you and our fellow men.
R. Make us truly sorry, and increase our love for you and for
our brothers.
—Speak to us, Holy Spirit, in the church and in our inmost
hearts, and increase our desire for all that is right and good.
We are sorry that we have offended you by our disobedience and
our hardness of heart.
R. Make us truly sorry, and increase our love for you and for our
brothers.

Minister:
    Let us now turn to God in prayer, that he may forgive us our
sins and deliver us from evil. Our Father . . .

70 A hymn may be sung at this point, and the service concludes
with the following thanksgiving:

71 —God of consolation and Father of mercy, you forgive the sins
of those who confess to you.
R. We praise you and bless you.
—God of consolation and Father of mercy, you grant to those
who suffer a share in your Son's passion, which enables them
to work with him for the salvation of the world.
R. We praise you and bless you.
—God of consolation and Father of mercy, you love those who
are troubled and sorrowful. You give them the hope of salvation
and promise them eternal life.
R. We praise you and bless you.
—Let us pray: Great is your goodness, Lord, and infinite your
mercy. We thank you for the gifts you have given us, and pray
you look upon this family of yours, gathered together in the name
of your Son. Keep it safe in lively faith, and firm hope, with a
sincere love for you and for all men. Amen.

72 Instead of the prayer, the service may be concluded with a blessing:

—May the God of peace fill your hearts with all goodness, so that, being strengthened with divine hope and comfort, you may live according to his will and so come to find eternal salvation. May almighty God grant you this, and every blessing: The Father, the Son ✠ and the Holy Spirit. Amen.

73 Instead of dismissing the congregation, the minister and other visitors could spend some time in conversation with the patients.

Appendix III

Examination of Conscience

I The following schemes can be adapted or amplified according to local customs and different needs.

II As a preparation for the sacrament of penance, everyone should be required to consider the following:

> a Do I approach the sacrament of penance with a sincere desire to change my life? Am I striving for purification and a deeper friendship with God, or do I think of confession as a burden, and as something to be done as rarely as possible?
> b Have I forgotten to mention, or deliberately avoided mentioning any grave sins in former confessions?
> c Have I performed the penance that was required of me? Have I made reparation for any damage I may have done? Have I made a serious effort to live according to the gospel, which is what I undertook by my purpose of amendment?

III Everyone should examine his conscience in the light of the word of God.

A Jesus said, 'You must love the Lord your God with all your heart' (Matt. 22: 37).
1 Is my heart so turned to God that I love him above all things, to the extent of carrying out his commandments as a son should obey his father? Or do I think more of temporal things? Have I a right intention in what I undertake?
2 God has spoken to us through his Son. Have I a strong faith in God? Have I kept firmly to the doctrines of the church? Have I listened to the word of God? Have I attended to Christian instruction and catechism? Have I avoided anything dangerous to my faith? Have I fearlessly professed my faith in God and the church? Have I been willing to show myself a Christian in public as well as private life?
3 Have I said my morning and evening prayers? Is my prayer a real conversation with God in heart and mind, or just an exterior

observance? Have I offered up to God my work, my joys and sorrows? Do I turn to him in times of temptation?

4 Have I a true reverence and love for the name of God, or have I offended him through blasphemy or perjury? Have I been irreverent to the Blessed Virgin Mary or the saints?

5 Do I observe Sundays and feast days? Do I attend mass actively, attentively and devoutly? Have I obeyed the church's commandments regarding annual confession and Easter communion?

6 Do I perhaps worship other gods, that is to say things for which I care too much, or put too much trust in? Such things as money, superstition, spiritualism?

B Jesus said, 'This is my commandment: love one another as I have loved you' (John 15: 12).

1 Do I really love my fellow men, or do I use them for my own ends? Do I do anything to them that I would not wish to have done to myself? Have I given them grave scandal by any of my words or actions?

2 Consider whether you have contributed to the good of your family by being patient and truly loving. Do the children obey their parents? Do they honour them, and help them in their material and spiritual needs? Do the parents look after the Christian education of their children? Do they help them by their authority and good example? Are the husband and wife faithful to each other in their hearts, and in their behaviour with others?

3 Do I share my worldly goods with those who are less well off than myself? Do I, as far as I am able, defend those who are oppressed, and help the needy? Or do I look down on people because they are poor, or weak, or old, or of different race?

4 Am I faithful in my life to the mission I undertook in confirmation? Do I share in the apostolate, in works of charity, in the life of my parish? Have I given any help to the needs of the church and the world? Have I prayed for these needs, e.g. for the unity of the church, for peace and justice, for the propagation of the gospel?

5 Have I a care for the prosperity and the good of the community I live in, or do I think only of myself? Do I do my share in promoting charity and concord, justice and decency? Have I fulfilled my duties as a citizen? Have I paid my taxes?

6 Am I honest, industrious and just at work, offering my services out of love for my fellow men? Have I given just remuneration

to those who work for me? Have I kept my promises and been faithful to my contracts?

7 Have I shown due respect and obedience to legitimate authority?

8 If I exercise authority or occupy some position, do I use these for my own good, or for the good of others in a spirit of service?

9 Have I kept to the truth, or have I told lies? Have I been guilty of calumny, detraction, rash judgment? Have I done wrong to anyone by betraying a secret?

10 Have I injured anyone physically? Have I injured anyone's good name or honour, or anything that belongs to my neighbour? Have I caused loss or damage to anyone? Have I procured abortion or persuaded anyone else to procure it? Have I taken anyone to law with hatred in my heart? Have I cut myself off from others through anger, quarrelling, enmity? Have I neglected, through selfishness, to help anyone unjustly accused?

11 Have I stolen? Have I coveted? Have I damaged something belonging to another? Have I made restitution, and repaired any damage I may have done?

12 If I have suffered any injury, have I accepted it peaceably for the love of Christ, and been forgiving? Or have I shown hatred and harboured a desire for revenge?

C Jesus said, 'Anybody who receives my commandments and keeps them will be one who loves me' (John 14: 21).

1 What is the basic direction of my life? Am I animated by the hope of eternal life? Have I tried to make progress in the spiritual life through prayer, meditation, reading the word of God, receiving the sacraments and mortifying myself? Have I tried to overcome my vices, passions and evil inclinations, such as envy and gluttony? Have I rebelled against God and despised my fellow men through pride and arrogance? Have I imposed my will on others, and ignored their rights and their freedom?

2 What use have I made of my time, my powers, my gifts, the 'talents' I have received from God? Have I used these things to make myself more perfect in God's sight, or have I been lazy and slothful?

3 Have I patiently put up with sufferings and misfortunes? What have I done in the way of mortification to make up for 'what is lacking in the suffering of Christ'? Have I observed the law of fasting and abstinence?

4 Have I kept guard over my body and senses? Have I been

modest and chaste, as befits a temple of the Holy Spirit, called to the glory of the resurrection? The sacrament of marriage is a sign of God's love in the world. Have I committed fornication? Have I been immodest in word or thought, impure desires or actions? Have I given way to my desires? Have I attended any kind of entertainment, or done any reading that was offensive to Christian decency? Have I encouraged others to sin by indecent behaviour? Have I observed the moral law in marriage?

5 Have I acted against my conscience through fear or hypocrisy?

6 Have I tried to live my life in the liberty of a true son of God, following the law of the Spirit, or am I a slave to my passions?